Pages From the Book of My Life

-A Translated Memoir-

by Hagop Abadjian

Pages From the Book of My Life
A translated memoir

By Hagop Abadjian

Copyright © 2021

El Design Creative

All rights reserved. No part of this book may be reproduced in any form by any electronic or mechanical means including photocopying, recording, or information storage and retrieval without permission in writing.

ISBN-13: 978-0-578-33171-3

Translated from Armenian to English by Lale Pakraduni
Edited by Nathalie C. Karimian, Ed.D.
Cover art and interior layout design by Eleen A. Abadjian

Give feedback on the book at:
eldesign@gmail.com

First Edition

Printed in the U.S.A

to
all who have fought for survival

Translator's note

Projects such as translating Mr. Abadjian's journey was one of the most fulfilling works I have taken on. Being a descendent of Armenian Genocide survivors, listening to and reading such stories have had a profound impact on my own journey, as I have found myself as an Armenian woman, keen on keeping the generational promise of never forgetting the atrocity Ottoman perpetrators committed against my people. Translating such stories and making them accessible to everyone, regardless of their ability to read Armenian, is imperative to the endurance of our history and people. This work would have not been possible without the cooperation, collaboration and guidance of Arin Chekijian a comrade in Beirut, Lebanon and Nare Kalemkerian, a freelance translator in Lebanon as well. The encouragement parents, brother and my love pushed me to take on this project. Most importantly however, my participation in this project would not be even conceivable without the eighteen years I've spent at Yeghishe Manoukian College, in Lebanon, where I mastered both Armenian and English.

Lale Pakradounian is a Phd Student of International and Comparative politics at the School of Social Sciences, Policy and Evaluation at Claremont Graduate University. She has been an active member of community organizations in Lebanon where she grew up and in Los Angeles after she moved to California to pursue graduate studies.

Granddaughter's note
As the last Abadjian in my family, I felt a sense of responsibility and obligation to my grandfather and to my family to have his memoir translated. Unfortunately, during the 2020 Artsakh War, history repeated itself. I was reminded that many around the globe still do not know that Armenia exists and, it is the lack of this knowledge, that gives enemies an upper hand. That inspired me to translate and publish my grandfather's memoir in hopes to share the struggle and survival of the Armenian people with a larger audience.
It is important for me to pass down my family's history, not only to the world, but also to my children and future generations.
I would like to thank everyone that was part of this project and to those still fighting for freedom and justice around the world.
Eleen Abadjian

Editor's note
As I worked on "Pages From the Book of My Life," it became increasingly important to make sure Hagop Abadjian's voice and purpose came through just right. I cross-checked with the original Armenian version to better understand Abadjian and the feelings he wanted to convey, to make sure as little as possible was lost in translation. Editing this book also took me on a research journey. In order to fulfill Abadjian's purpose in providing historical records for the Armenian Genocide, I searched for the original historical documents, accurate names of people and locations, and even did some cultural research for certain sections. This biographical work is representative of the bravery and nuances that shape each Armenian story. It was a pleasure to be part of bringing Abadjian's incredible story to a larger audience.

Nathalie C. Karimian is an educator and researcher. She received her Educational Doctorate from the University of Southern California. Her work specializes in educational psychology and the Armenian-American experience.

PAGES FROM THE BOOK OF MY LIFE

Contents

Introduction	3
Part One	7
Part Two	19
Part Three	31
Part Four	49
Part Five	65
Part Six	79
Part Seven	93
Part Eight	105

Introduction

Hagop Abadjian was the son of Mardiros Abadjian who lived in Yoghunoluk, Musa Dagh. He was born in Urfa. He spent a part of his life in Musa Dagh and was an active participant in the region's resistance against the Turkish forces who were deporting Armenians from their homes during World War I. With Franz Werfel's famous work, "The Forty Days of Musa Dagh," the resistance was memorialized. The reality was as striking as told by the author.

If this work, "Pages from the Book of My Life," was only about the resistance of Musa Dagh, it would be just as interesting. Instead, it provides additional information about the battle—adding to Dikran Antreassian's "Memories," Iskenderian's "Suetia's Revolt," Boursalian's "The Battle of Musa Dagh"— and enriches the story of one of our most courageous fights.

With this work, a Musa Dagh native speaks about incredible perseverance, which could serve diaspora communities. Indeed, some of the events may not arouse interest today, but could one day provide valuable historical perspective. As the past has shown, history is forgotten when people are indifferent. We live in a time when the recording of a minor event may be imperative for the enlightenment of future issues.

The author has committed to write about these events, including information about several regions that are part of our people's recent past. We find it imperative and useful for coming generations to print such works.

We should welcome and appreciate such contributions to our history and culture. There comes a time when some of these works become irreplaceable literary and historic treasures. Presently, praiseworthy work is being done in the homeland in this regard. In the Armenian Diaspora, many such treasures are likely being destroyed, especially handwritten letters of those who have had immense influence on the cultural and political life of the community.

The author of this work is a well-known translator. In 1960, The "Armenia" newspaper in Buenos Aires published his translation of Paul Ilton's "The Last Days of Sodom and Gomorrah." In 1950, his work, "The Secret of the Sands," was published in Beirut, Lebanon. Nowadays, in Canada, he remains dedicated to our language and literature.

It is with that vigor that he gave us the story of the Battle of Musa Dagh and the heroes who, more than 5,000 in count, gained worldwide attention in 1915. They moved to Port Said and became the main reason for the establishment of the Eastern Legion. They lost 600 courageous volunteers and took part in the Battle of Arara and invaded Cilicia.

The history and the life of the Armenians of the past 50 years presented in this autobiography, "Pages From the Book of My Life," is worthy of our attention.

Vartan Kevorkian

Buenos Aries, October 25, 1972

In Lieu of an Introduction

As I filled the pages of my autobiography, "Pages From the Book of My Life," I had one thing in mind, to describe a life of three quarters of a century. I would be wrong to say that my story is the fate of every single Armenian.

I've had a couple turning points in my life that change the course of my life. I survived in 1895, during the dark days of the Hamidian massacres, and later in the Armenian Genocide of 1915, during the horrid days of the forced deportations.

Like me, many Armenians who survived the Genocide experienced an odyssey. I recounted these events in writing to serve as an example for others to record their stories for the sake of history.

During the journey of my life and within the chapters of this book, I have given space to specific works without altering any of their words. Some of those works described their disbelief at the atrocities faced by our people during the Armenian Genocide while others have described the battles.

Today, living on foreign lands, we are aware of our past, communally remembering to keep the visionary soul of Armenians alive. I am certain that we will continue preserving our culture and nation. However, if our circumstances harden our hearts, oh, then may God help us.

But, the harp of hope still has a single string remaining.

M.L.

Toronto, 1970

PAGES FROM THE BOOK OF MY LIFE

Part One

Just before the start of summer, two horsemen left from Yoghunoluk to the villages of Musa Dagh. That morning, they were passing through the road that led to Antioch. The first rays of the sunrise were visible when the two men passed through the shallow waters of the Karachay and headed towards the town.

With great caution, the men crossed the bridge left by the Romans over the Orontes River, avoiding the guards stationed at the head of the bridge who sometimes questioned travelers from Suetia. Their first order of business was to check the schedule of the caravan leaving for Aleppo and make arrangements to leave with it. To arrive in Aleppo, the two travelers would need to spend a night in Kirik Khan, which was an inn, and later in Afrin.

It was 1891. The caravan was to leave the next morning. A hound, Sultan Abdul Hamid II, was sitting on the throne of the Ottoman Empire. In order to avoid creating suspicion in Antioch, the two men spent the day in the Armenian church of the town. They had left their horses and their trivial items at an inn overlooking the river.

The next morning, the two young men joined the caravan with their horses. The caravan was headed by a muleteer from Aintab. In the afternoon, the caravan rested in Kirik Khan. It seemed like a large number of Armenians had been established there from prehistoric times because several stores were owned by Armenians. It was an unusual intersection there, on the road to Iskenderun. After spending the night there, they continued their voyage to reach Aleppo by the third afternoon.

Aleppo was one of Turkey's governorates. For years now, Hovhannes Nigoghossian, a local of Yoghunoluk, had established himself there and had married a local Arabic-speaking woman. When they arrived at the village, it was easy for them to find their compatriot, who was known as Vanis Nikolay.

Our two travelers, Mardiros Abadjian and Boghos Dmlekian, were interested in putting their comb-making skills to work in a city as big as Aleppo, where Armenians had lived since old times. They had the necessary items with them at all times. They were dissuaded from staying in Aleppo because the language of the city was Arabic and that was going to make it difficult for them to be successful in terms of business. Given the political concerns of the time, their compatriot failed in convincing them to not move on to the Armenian Highlands. Mardiros and Boghos decided to go further east.

In those days, transportation with wheels was not available. Only once every two weeks, a caravan would set off to Mardin and Dikranagerd. They found a caravan that was headed east. On a beautiful day, the caravan headed out. After traveling through harsh conditions, they reached the Arabic-speaking city of Mardin at the bank of the Euphrates River. Mardin's population was comprised of ancient Assyrians. They felt out of place and decided to visit the Armenian church. Boghos liked the city and decided to settle down there. He later met the Protestant reverend and married his daughter.

Mardiros, however, was eager to go further to Dikranagerd and the Armenian Highlands, to Bitlis and Van. He parted ways with his friend and headed to Dikranagerd. Wherever he passed through, he used his trade to work. Given the Hamidian regime's ambivalence towards foreign travelers, he wanted to give the impression that he did not have any special interests as a traveler.

He stayed in Dikranagerd for a month and met local Armenians through the Armenian church there. Concerned about his travels and safety, he gathered information about the Armenian Highlands. He was passionate about his homeland and yearned to see the city of Van and its sea, which was a hub for Armenians.

He traveled with Kurdish and Armenian muleteers from the city of Sasun and reached Bitlis. He realized that the way of life for Armenians in Sasun was completely different from those of Antioch . After some time however, he became accustomed to the Armenian dialect of the region. It was a completely new region for him and there were no craftsmen who worked with combs there.

After staying there for a while, he moved on to Van. The first month of summer had already passed when he arrived to the city he had yearned for so long. Mardiros had heard about the Sea of Van at his village and, today, he could see the vast waters of Van with his own eyes. Here too, he sought Armenians who listened to his accounts of Cilician Armenia with great interest.

He was discreet and did not want to stay too long to avoid getting arrested as a foreigner.

An Armenian caravanner from Sasun took Mardiros through Erzurum, Severak, and Urfa, reaching Dikranagerd after two days of travel. It was the end of fall and winter was not too far.

The City of Urfa

In Urfa, formerly known as Yetesia, there lived over 25,000 Armenians. Having come from Aleppo, Mardiros noticed similarities in the customs and ways of life to the adjacent Antioch. He decided to settle down there.

Mardiros was a Protestant and so, on the first Sunday, he went to the community center located a block from him and met with the local reverend, Hagop Abehayatian. He found the city's shopping center, located between the Armenian and Turkish neighborhoods, was best for his comb-making. He rented a store and started work. This eventually became a very successful endeavor for him.

The year was 1892.

The political environment was charged and there were fears that Sultan Hamid II was going to expand his hold to the Armenian population in the Eastern provinces. Mardiros still lived in a room he rented from an inn close to his shop and had already met Protestant Armenian families who he visited socially.

One day at a Sunday service, in a strange coincidence, he caught sight of a beautiful girl from the Yeranosian family and became mesmerized with her. After the service, Mardiros followed the girl and found where she lived. The next day, he asked the Reverend who the girl was that lived in that house.

"Yes, my son," the Reverend answered, "that girl is part of the Yeranosian family, who are members of our community. I understand what you are saying, you have made a good choice. My son, if you wish to marry her, I will see to it at once."

"Reverend," he answered, "I have already told you that I am a native of Musa Dagh and the son of a Protestant family. If I marry here, I will finally put an end to my nomadic life. If I had stayed in our villages back home, I would have been a simple craftsman or a shepherd. Here, I have greater possibilities and can at least get some education. My dad is considered part of the wealthy class back home but it was against his beliefs to get an education. He used to say 'What's the worth of a hefty education? You need to stay here in the village and take care of the land.'"

Mardiros got married that same year. He fathered two sons. His first son passed away after only 10 months. The second was born in the fall of 1894 and named Hagop, after his grandfather.

This was my birth in Urfa.

***

Sultan Hamid II's cruel plans caused the political climate to worsen, bringing about the Hamidian massacres of 1894 to 1896.

My father, having experience in agriculture back home, had great knowledge in tree injection. One of the Turkish Aghas in Urfa had a friendly relationship with my father. He owned a grove nearby where he invited my father to inject his trees one day. There, the Turkish Agha referenced the ongoing political turmoil, including the plans of the Sultan to exterminate the Armenian race. He made a friendly suggestion to my father to leave Urfa and return to his birthplace in Antioch where the prospects of a massacre were less. My father listened to his suggestion shortly after the visit.

Fall 1894 was coming to an end.

I was merely a couple months old when my father secretly informed my mother of his plan to leave Urfa. He suggested they leave this city together to go back to his birthplace, Yoghunoluk. Though my mother protested at first, she was finally convinced by my father's insistence and her brothers' promises that she could return to Urfa after the massacres.

Life was completely different during these times. The only trustworthy method for traveling was with caravans led by muleteers. The road from Urfa to Aleppo and Antioch was an eight-day voyage, traveling 10 hours a day. One morning, my parents bid farewell to their loved ones and were on their way to Aleppo. As my mother carried me, my parents traveled through Aleppo for nine days. They finally reached Musa Dagh's Yoghunoluk village.

Hearing that Mardiros had returned home, many villagers rushed to greet the tall young man who had left home years ago. My mother used to tell us that, because of this joyous occasion, rounds of ammunition were fired as well. My grandfather and grandmother were used to the atmosphere and ways of village life and so they were very happy to have their prodigal son return.

It was here where I came to know the world and enjoyed a great childhood. I don't remember much from the early days of my childhood. Our home was next to the Protestant church where other Protestant families lived as well. Our homes were close to one another. I have sparing memories from these days.

This feeling lasted until 1902, when my father passed away at the age of 37, leaving behind a 28-year-old widow and three underaged children.

I was seven years old when my father passed away. I saw the funeral procession and couldn't understand why they put him in a coffin, sealed it, and took him away.

***

Let us return to Urfa for a moment. Sinister news reached us from the massacres of Urfa. The massacres had devastated the village, killing more than 5,000 souls. Thousands were burnt in the main church. Reverend Hagop Abehayatian was shot in front of his house. Thankfully, both of my mother's brothers, Hagop and Hovhannes, had survived by some miracle. Though, they had lost their homes to looting.

Urfa now looked like a ghost town. My father visited the city shortly before his passing. He was happy to know that his brothers-in-law had survived, but the furniture and other items he had left there had been looted. Thus, he abandoned the idea of returning to Urfa one day and returned to his birthplace.

***

When I returned to my father's home in 1914, I was reminded of the strategic location of Yoghunoluk, in the green valley of the Orontes River. Behind it, on the southern horizon of the valley, was Mount Casius, also known as Jebel Aqra.

There were two houses in my grandfather's yard, one of which was remodeled by my father. My father's passing left a big hole in the family. My grandfather was concerned with who would take care of us three little orphans and how we would live. Mourning sometimes passes quickly, especially when the survivors are concerned with the future. My mother wrote to her brother, mourning the loss of her husband and disclosing the unstable situation she was facing. She was worried that, if her lovely children grew up in this village, they would become shepherds or common workers.

A few months after my father's death, my uncle Hagop, joined a caravan with his own horse and arrived in Aleppo and then Antioch. He ran into some villagers from Musa Dagh and learned the way to the village. He traveled to Suetia and then Yoghunoluk. My mother was overjoyed when she saw her beloved brother.

At the time, Turkish law held that, when a parent passed away, their children couldn't inherit from the grandfather who was still alive. The board of the local Protestant church quickly pushed my grandfather to ignore that unlawful tradition and had him sign an agreement. Years later, however, when we were older, we returned to our father's home and found that this agreement had been lost during World War I.

After discussing the topic, my mother and uncle agreed to send me to Urfa with my uncle. It was imperative, however, to ask my grandfather's opinion on the matter.

"Grandpa Abadji," said my uncle, "it pains me and I mourn the loss of your son Mardiros. Though, as a grandfather, you are obliged to take care of these orphans. This village is located at one of the ends of the world. There are no opportunities for them to receive a proper education here. Please allow me to take the eldest, Hagop, with me, so I can take care of him and provide him with an education as his father would have done. As for my sister and the other two children, I will make future arrangements for them to come and live in an Armenian-populated city like Urfa."

The reverend of the village and the Protestant preacher were also present during this conversation. My grandfather considered it and agreed. He also promised to regularly send five Ottoman gold coins to my uncle in order to help with the finances.

My mother was happy that we were going to leave village-life for a new, still Armenian, environment.

To Urfa

My mother's brother stayed in Yoghunoluk for a week. One morning, long before dawn, he put me on his horse and we left for Antioch. I vaguely remember our stay at an inn in Antioch. Someone with ill wishes had told my grandfather that he hadn't made the right decision in allowing his grandson to leave, causing some conflict. One day, while I was waiting alone in our room at the inn, my uncle was arrested. He was able to bribe his way out it and was set free. It was past noon when he came with the caravan. We set out for Aleppo, hoping to reach the first hotel before nightfall. That night we stayed at Kirik Khan.

We reached Aleppo three days after we had left the village. We had to rest for a couple of days before continuing our voyage to Urfa. We still needed three days to reach the village. When we reached the Euphrates River, a young man from Urfa, who had been on the voyage with us, decided to swim across the river. Instead, we took our horse on the boat and crossed to the other side to reach Berejik.

The city of Berejik used to be a fortress in ancient times. It was south of Rumkale. There were many Armenians living there. We had to leave again in the early hours of the morning, knowing that we were 20 hours away from our final destination.

It took us a week to finally reach my uncle's home in Urfa. At this point, the seven years I had spent in Musa Dagh seemed like a dream. My mother and younger siblings joined us a couple of months later. I reached my teenage years in the city of Urfa, which had been a completely new environment for me. It was hard for me to understand the spoken dialect, since I was familiar with the dialect spoken in Musa Dagh. It took me a short while, however, to assimilate and start speaking like them. My uncle took me to church on the first Sunday there and then to school the next day.

Let me make one or two remarks about Urfa. This city had been the old city of Yetesia, which was located north of the fields of Mesopotamia. The area was more similar to highlands. The city had been fortified by a stone wall and boulders still remained in some places. The Armenian neighborhood was located on the skirts of Til Fidur Hill and was almost completely detached from the Turkish neighborhoods, which stretched from the main shopping center to Kharan.

Urfa had also been the first cradle of Christianity. Who doesn't know of King Apgar and the image of Edessa and Saint Thaddeus' mission to Urfa? It was here that the first saints, hermits, and theorists paved the way to Christianity with their sacrifices.

The contemporary history of Urfa began from 1908 to 1915, lasting until current times. Previously, it had been where the older generation had spent their youth and it was full of their memories. In 1908, the Ottoman Constitution gave Urfa the opportunity to be in contact with the rest of the region, give importance to education, and dive into the world of art. The city started progressing quickly and, in a very short time, Armenian patriotism and education peaked.

After reaching Urfa, we stayed with our uncle Hagop and his large family. He took care of us like a father.

Part Two

Life in Urfa

It wasn't possible to continue living like this. My mother became our guardian angel. She found a job working at the embroidery factory founded by the American missionary workers. She was able to make a humble living by embroidering napkins. We moved to a one-bedroom home that was close to our relatives.

Some suggested that we, the orphans, go to the American orphanage, which was established after the Hamidian massacres in 1895. My mother, however, would say "God deprived me from my husband and gave me the responsibility to keep my three children in their mother's arms." She didn't believe that children raised in an orphanage could have a healthy upbringing.

Urfa became our home though we had to live off limited means for 13 years. Everything was affordable and plentiful even though our only income was my mother's humble work and my grandfather's limited financial assistance.

Here, without mentioning all the cruel details, I unwillingly move to the year 1908. I was a teenager, barely 14 years old. Based on our circumstances, we ended up living in several different homes.

After the Cilician massacres, my grandfather from Musa Dagh, invited me to visit my paternal home and I was compelled to go. My mother was a wise woman and, before leaving, had arranged the paperwork identifying her guardianship over us through a lawyer.

After the proper arrangements were made, my mother and I left for Musa Dagh and my sister and brother were left under the care of my uncles. When we reached the village and my grandfather saw his eldest grandchild had grown, he showered me with lavish love and care. After staying there for an entire month, my mother and I returned to Urfa through the same route.

Much like my mother's brother had foreseen, our settling in Urfa proved to be advantageous. I was given the opportunity to attend elementary school and then the boys' high school. The school's principal, Khoren Krikorian, was an alumnus of the Euphrates College in Kharpert. There were two other educators from the American "Central Turkey" College in Aintab. Naturally, Turkish was the official language of instruction but, Armenian was as important. English was the only foreign language of instruction. In 1911, Dikran Haroutounian and Setrag Sahagian were also part of our faculty. Urfa also had a high school for girls. The pastor of the parish was Father Asadour Yeghoian.

As such, everything was normal. We had our graduation ceremony in 1911. My classmates were Garabed Kavafian, Yesayi Attarian, Garabed Keverian, Hovhannes Najarian, and Barkev Yegenian.

As the eldest child in our household, I had to worry about our livelihood. After graduating, I asked my mother's brother Hovhannes for guidance. He suggested I learn the craft of comb-making from him.

We had a distant relative who was a pharmacist in a large Ottoman hospital. They invited me to study pharmacy rather than the dull work of comb-making. The hospital was located outside of the Armenian quarters. It was a 30-minute walk. I liked this opportunity because I was pursuing a career. However, I barely survived two weeks. Many times, I had to survive on a small piece of bread and some cheese for lunch. The lack of food didn't allow me to continue. So, I resigned my wish to pursue pharmacy and decided to pursue comb-making with my uncle.

I should mention that my uncle had learned comb-making from my father and occupied the same shop as he had in the central market. In the market, almost all the shop owners were Armenian. The baker was Armenian, the farrier was Armenian, the painter was Baghsar Agha, the kebab cook was Sarkis, the man who sold nuts was Levon, the barber was Jerahian, the tinsmith was Krikor, the gunsmith was Hovhannes, and many other Armenians made up the merchants and artisans of the market. The Turks were not craftspeople but simple shopkeepers; some made wooden saddles. Armenians were the craftspeople. After the Hamidian massacres of 1895, the new generation had risen from the ashes and were successful in every field.

I made great progress in comb-making. My uncle was very happy and paid me two and a half coins per week.

The First Major Turning Point

Nevertheless, destiny had a different plan for me. One day, the church's head secretary, Effendi Soghomon Knajian, visited our store and made quite a strange suggestion. The church had an educational association for its studious but needy youth. Mr. Knajian said, "Mr. Yeranosian, it is a pity that this boy, who is one of the best students in our high school, practices this job. We will cover his school expenses so he can study at the American "Central Turkey" College in Aintab. You, as the person in charge, will sign a promissory note that he will pay his debt in two years by serving as a teacher in our school."

My uncle was an educated man. He easily accepted the man's advice. He agreed and also promised to gift me money for expenses. I was pleased that I was granted the opportunity to pursue higher education.

The next day I went to Mr. Knajian's office, which was in the building of the American missionary. He handed me a letter to give to the president of the college. He encouraged me by giving me some money for minor expenses as well. "We expect that you will happily pursue your education according to the arrangements. May God be with you," said Mr. Knajian.

My mother was very happy about this opportunity, although she was sad that her eldest son would be away from home for two years. She made whatever preparations she could, procuring underclothes and a coat for wintertime.

This was the first major turning point in my life.

To Aintab

At the beginning of each school year, muleteers from Adiyaman would come to Urfa to take the students to the American "Central Turkey" College in Aintab. We were 13 students, among which there were female students who were going to the girls' college. We were set to depart in the afternoon because the weather was quite hot in mid-September. We had to arrive at Berejik the next day at noon, through a 20-hour journey. Relatives and friends had come to wish us a safe journey. While leaving, my Uncle Hagop told me, "Hagop, I brought you to Urfa as a child. Now, you are walking on the road of life. Be a faithful soldier of Christ and live as an Armenian."

The caravan set off. Many of the students kept looking back to see their loved ones, who were waving handkerchiefs. Among our group were Dikran Haroutounian, Kevork Takvorian, Garabed Keverian, Yesayi Attarian, Krikor Madarian and, among other girls, Gassia Madarian.

We barely reached Berejik the next evening. Nine years earlier, I had passed through this town with my uncle.

The City of Aintab

The city of Aintab was 3,000 feet above sea level. On the west, it was 75 miles from Iskenderun Bay and 40 miles from Antioch. The city was surrounded by vineyards and pistachio trees. It had almost no large expanse to plant crops. The vineyards and trees were separated by stone walls.

There were two unpaved state roads. One came from the east, from Malatia, and crossed the north, reaching Kilis, Aleppo, and the region including the Mediterranean, Antioch, and

Iskenderun. The other road started from the west and reached south, arriving at Marash and Zeitun. Both were covered in dust and would cause dust clouds from the wind.

When a traveler took the main road and went to the right, above the coast, he could see the American "Central Turkey" College's spacious yard that was surrounded by a three meter stone fence. In this yard, there were two main buildings: the dormitory for students who stayed overnight and the building for students who came to school each day. There were also the houses of the president and doctor. On the opposite hill of the boys' college, were the main buildings for the girl's college and the hospital. The chief physician of the hospital was Dr. Shepard.

At the end of one street, through the winding narrow streets of the city, we could see the dome of Saint Mary's Church. Although the Middle East was producing wood and timber for construction, Armenian architecture had long preferred to build with sandstone and other hard stones. Generally, the houses had flat roofs and small yards. Some signs showed that the city had bordered the Armenian Kingdom of Cilicia, where 25 to 30 thousand Armenians had lived.

Until the Armenian Genocide of 1915, Aintab was considered an important center for Armenians. The majority of the Armenians there spoke Turkish, even those who had attended college and taken advanced courses in the Armenian language.

The official language of the American "Central Turkey" College in Aintab was Turkish but the advanced scientific courses were taught in English. The institution was American but, in fact, had a definitive Armenian spirit. For half a century, intellectual Armenians graduated from this college and pursued their education at the American University of Beirut, going on to work in scientific and other fields.

Six centuries ago, when Turks from the Mongol tribes invaded Asia Minor with their destructive criminal instincts and turned everything into chaos, the flourishing cities were nearly destroyed and their populations murdered. To recover, they needed an easy religion, so they accepted Islam and turned it into a means to their ends.

The cities on the other side of the Euphrates River were able to preserve their language while those on the Western side became Turkish-speakers. It was obvious that the population had been forced to speak only in Turkish. And, if that was not enough, the crooked Turks also settled in the prosperous cities and villages and enjoyed the products made by the Armenian people.

It is horrifying to think that, today, after the Armenian Genocide of 1915, the hundreds of churches there are being used as farms or jails and the church bells are silent.

***

In Berejik, we stayed at a hotel on the riverbank. Early the next morning, we crossed the Euphrates River and reached the other side using special boats and pack animals. It was really pleasant to travel with a group. We sang patriotic songs. I only remember one of them, "Sleep, My Baby" by Aharonian. I remembered the day my uncle Hagop and I had crossed those vast waters.

We made it to Nizib by nighttime. Nizib was a small town surrounded by trees. We went to a nearby garden to buy apricots and peaches. We were very tired so we went to bed early to continue our journey the next morning.

We were 10 hours from the college. We made it to our destination at noon. Students were arriving from everywhere. Some came from faraway places like Adiyaman, Malatia, Dikranagerd, the distant Van, and western regions such as Hasanbeyli, Kesab, and Kirik Khan. The newcomers from the east had spent the night outdoors on the college grounds and taken medicine for malaria. Our blankets and pillows were left out under the scorching sun until a place was prepared for us in one of the bedrooms. Since it was Wednesday, there were no classes. All the new students took entrance exams to determine their courses.

The American "Central Turkey" College felt like a family. Each morning students from the town would come. Besides Turkish, Armenian language and literature were taught. Theology students also took Classical Armenian language, taught by Nshan Baleozian. Natural Sciences was taught by the white-haired Alexan Bezdjian, History by Zenop Bezdjian, Mathematics by Loutfi Babikian, Botany by Jessy Matossian, and Music and Instruments by Hagop Youvezian. The college's president was Dr. John Merrill, and his secretary was Hovhannes Hasserjian.

It was 1912.

Professor Alexan Bezdjian died of cardiac arrest. The school closed for the day and we attended his funeral. It was almost the end of the school year. I received an invitation from my grandfather to spend the summer at Yoghunoluk. My fellow classmates from Kesab and I headed to Antioch in a horse carriage. I reached the village.

In Musa Dagh, I loved being in an Armenian environment

again and enjoyed the summer fruits. The summer flew by and I returned to Aintab in the fall to continue my education. As a result of the former school year's exams, I was placed in fourth, or freshman, class. The students who had vacationed in Urfa returned, along with some new ones: Garabed Attarian, Georgi Tashjian, and Garabed Tchboukjian.

My Uncle Hovhannes used to write to me from Urfa to update me about my mother, sister, and brother. At the end of that school year, I received an official letter from Soghomon Knajian inviting me to teach at the boys' high school in Urfa for the 1913-1914 school year. My salary was set to two Ottoman gold coins, half of which would be paid to the educational association, as repayment for my loan.

Returning to Urfa

After the graduation ceremony in June 1913, my fellow-classmates from Urfa and I returned to our birthplace. At the entrance of the town, my mother, sister, brother, and relatives had gathered to welcome us. My mother was searching for me as I was standing next to her. I had become an adult.

At the beginning of the 1913 school year, I started teaching at the boys' high school. My colleagues were Avedis Avedian from the Euphrates College in Kharpert and Mihran Balikian from the American "Central Turkey" College. The head of elementary was Garabed Keverian. I was teaching history and mathematics. Once a week, the teachers would take turns leading discussions before the start of our classes. It was overwhelming for me to speak for even 10 minutes.

I was 18 years old and I felt like a young adult now.

Armenian nationalism was growing in town. The spiritual leader of the Apostolic community was Pastor A. Kalenderian, a liberal nationalist priest. He had founded an educational association comprised of teachers from the Evangelical and Apostolic schools. He had also used his musical knowledge to form a choir and organize a concert, which was a novelty for the large Armenian community.

It was 1914. It was clear that an educational and cultural movement had begun.

An athletic association was founded. Regular rehearsals took place on Saturdays in the gymnasium. Theatrical performances were planned by prominent individuals. The first play was "St. Vartan's Battle," in which Dr. Armenag Abehayatian played the role of Vartan. He was the son of Reverend Hagop Abehayatian, who was martyred in 1895. The second play was "Ani is Sold," which was about Armenian royal life. Our teacher, Mr. Avedis Avedian, had turned this story into a play.

Urfa did not have a theater. The yard of the Evangelical school was big enough. Therefore, they set up huge tents and arranged a theater. This play generated a lot of enthusiasm. People attended in big numbers, and so did state officials.

However, the global political environment was murky and on the verge of erupting. A storm was approaching. This year, the graduation ceremonies for the boys' and girls' high schools took place in the church.

It was June 1914.

My brother Armenag, who was four years younger than me, was working at my uncle's comb-making shop. He came home one night and said, "Did you hear Brother? They are distributing sealed envelopes in the streets. It seems there is going to be a draft. There are rumors of war approaching."

Some were ready to enlist as soldiers and had already left for Aleppo. That period was agonizing.

Part Three

Returning to My Ancestral Home

We received a letter from Musa Dagh that week. Since we were not considered young anymore, my uncle was inviting us to live with their family in our paternal home. At the same time, since I was at the age of military service, he reminded me to settle the case with the college administration and whoever else I needed to settle it with.

After asking my mother's opinion, I considered my uncle's invitation. It was not difficult to make the decision for myself alone but, leaving my mother, sister and brother in Urfa would not be a good idea. This way, we would all be leaving Urfa together. The arrangement seemed difficult since we had already gotten used to life in Urfa. Nevertheless, we took the step, believing it might pave new roads for us. Day by day, we packed our belongings, leaving some of our furniture to our relatives. At that time, our house was adjacent to the church.

During those days, I did not know why but, I anticipated disaster would strike soon and leave most of our relatives homeless. I went to the hill of Tilfidu for a final view of the city. I felt as though I would never see the city where I spent my youth again!

The image of the farewell still lingers in my memory. Upon leaving, I had a feeling that all the relatives we were leaving would soon become victims. And so, it happened a year later. Only my cousin, the son of my maternal Uncle Hovhannes, survived, while staying with Arabs.

We reached Aleppo. It was the Sunday of Vartavar, a religious festival dating back to pagan times. At the church, I had the chance to meet the dean of the American "Central Turkey" College in Aintab, Dr. Merrill. Taking advantage of the opportunity, I asked him, "As you may know, I'm currently in my sophomore year. Is there any chance that I can skip my military service?"

He answered, "As much as I know my dear, sophomores will be exempt from military service. Make your arrangements and come to college. Leave the rest to God!"

Also, before leaving Urfa, I had met Mr. Leslie, an American missionary. I had asked him to find a sponsor for my studies, promising that I would travel to the United States in 1917 to pursue higher education. Since I was leaving Urfa, the educational association could no longer help me. I was told Mr. Leslie found a sponsor to take care of my expenses.

Both of these promises were very encouraging at the time. However, I would later learn that they were based on false hopes.

After staying at our relative's, Hovhannes Nigoghossian's, place in Aleppo, we continued our journey to Antioch, reaching our destination 13 days after leaving Urfa. It was great that the time we lived in Urfa was a large part of our lives!

That summer, I socialized with the Armenian Revolutionary Federation members of Yoghunoluk. I had already been going to the House of Chengents, which was the Armenian Revolutionary Federation's club. There, speeches given by the well-known revolutionary intellectual, Haroutioun Der Khorenian, largely shaped my nationalist views. This was exactly what I had been searching for, courageous youth, such as Stephan Kibourian, Movses Der Kalousdian, Setrag Boursalian, Serop Sherbetjian, Jabra Khehoian, and others, with whom I became good friends.

One day, Stephan Kibourian said, "A world war will start in Europe. Let's see what impact it will have for Armenians."

Poor guy! That fall, he had left for college and then was sent to Constantinople as a soldier, only to die from a ruthless disease.

My Last School Term (1914-1915)

World War I erupted. It was a sensible decision for me to go to Aintab and continue my higher education. My grandfather had generously given me five gold coins for my educational expenses. In the beginning of September, I went to Antioch and headed to college safely with the muleteers. After finishing the last two years of my schooling and receiving my diploma, I wanted to pursue higher education in the United States of America. Although this was a great plan, it didn't turn out as such.

At the beginning of 1915, Turkey was in a state of war. I was attending school. I was only able to receive two letters from my uncle, Hovhannes, because our letters were screened. There were Turkish students at the college who were studying the Armenian language. It later became evident that they were doing so because they had been assigned to screen our letters. They also probably caused the death of some of the Armenians in the Genocide.

After weathering a tough winter, we welcomed spring with joy. We heard about the war on the western front. Britain and France had declared war against Turkey and Turkey was heading towards Egypt through Palestine.

One afternoon, after school, I headed to the city with a student from Urfa. A big feast was taking place that day. Rioters with banners broke out on the street next to the Catholic church, shouting "We occupied the Suez Canal!" With them, they dragged a British flag through the dirt.

When I was a child, we had come to Musa Dagh and my father had registered for my birth certificate there. Because of that, a decree from Antioch was issued to draft me for military service. The military authorities of Aintab were also enlisting college students for military service.

It was a Wednesday. It so happened that I was near the entrance of the college courtyard when a soldier came to deliver a letter to the college president. The letter had a list of names attached. Maybe the soldier was ignorant because he asked me to deliver it to the President myself. I scanned the list and found my name. I was surprised to see it written as Yacoub instead of Hagop. I presumed the president would tell him that a student named Yacoub Veledi Mardir wasn't enrolled at the college. That presumption turned out to be true. Though, thereafter, I was in constant fear that the mix-up would be discovered.

Two weeks passed from that day.

The Major Turning Point that Changed the Course of My Life

It was a Wednesday night in the third week of March 1915. I was having nightmares because I felt like my last day at the college was approaching. The next morning, on March 18, I woke up and hurried to the cafeteria where the students would gather for lunch.

On my way there, one of my classmates suddenly grabbed my hand and asked, "What's happening? You look uneasy, as if something has happened. Do you have any news?"

I replied, "Nothing, dear George, I haven't been sleeping well and I feel as though today may be my last day at the college. May God grant us peace!"

We entered the cafeteria together for breakfast. I had no appetite whatsoever. Somehow, I could sense that I was at the brink of a major turning point of my life. I tried to appear as calm as I could so I wouldn't raise any suspicion.

***

Every morning at the college, the students, roughly 200 of us, would gather in the main hall to listen to the assigned professor for that day. Then, we would go to our classes.

After half a century has passed, I still remember the speech Professor Loutfi Babikian gave us that morning. The professor had selected the line from the Lord's Prayer, "Lead us not into temptation," as if he was prophesying the upcoming crisis. Alas, he couldn't escape the Genocide and fell victim with the other intellectuals of the century.

On another day, we had a Natural Sciences class with

Professor Daghlian. He was explaining mechanical engineering. Suddenly, there was a knock at the door and the President's assistant entered the classroom.

"Please send Mr. Hagop Abadjian to Dr. Merrill's office. It's urgent," he said.

Carrying my books, I followed him to the President's office. I noticed the President's worried expression. Pointing to the chairs, he asked me to sit. I sat and waited a couple of moments until he finished what he was writing.

"Do you know why I have asked you to come?" he asked.

"No," I answered. "but I know you wouldn't have asked me to leave class if it wasn't urgent."

"Listen, my son, regrettably, one week ago I received a list of all the students who should serve in the Turkish army. I was confused by the inaccuracy of some of the names and told them that they weren't our students. After your name is corrected, you should go to the enlistment office within eight days to arrange your military service."

This delivered a real shock to me. A minute later, I gathered myself and asked, "Oh my God! Do you remember the day I saw you in Aleppo and you reassured me that I would likely be exempt from military service?"

"I do, but no one could have forecasted that Turkey would join the war against the Allies. I advise you not to avoid military service!"

"But, are you liable for sending me to the Turkish authorities for military service?" I asked.

"What do you mean?" asked the President.

I replied, "Effective immediately, I ask you to no longer

consider me a student at your college and grant me the opportunity to return to my native village, Musa Dagh, where my relatives live. Another option would be to allow me to go to one of my relative's house in Aleppo tomorrow so that all trace of me is lost."

The President carefully studied my pale expression, just like a father would look at his son. "I seem confident that you will reach your native village safely. Please keep in mind that you need three days to reach it and it is very risky. If you have a relative in Aleppo, I advise you to go there rather than heading to Antioch. I allow you to leave. Without hesitation, finalize your tuition payments with the accountant. Leave the college tomorrow, early in the morning. We will tell the security guard to allow you to leave. Be careful! Do not tell anyone of this plan!"

This was the major turning point that changed the course of my life.

The Escape to Musa Dagh

As I left the President's office, a plan was already forming in my mind. Without hesitation, I went to the accountant's, Mr. Hasserjian's, office, to settle my tuition. I made sure I had enough money to reach Aleppo.

We had a break that afternoon. There was light rain. I felt I had made the right decision about leaving school.

It was March 15, 1915. It was a full moon. The dormitory lights of the American "Central Turkey" College were already off. A few of the students were already in bed. I was sitting alone on my bed looking out the window when a student from Urfa approached me.

"Why are you awake George?" I asked him.

"Let's go to the courtyard and get some fresh air," he said.

We went down and sat on one of the benches of the main building.

"What's your opinion about the war? How will it end?" I asked him.

"I don't have much to say but, I feel that, sooner or later, us Armenians are going to be deported because of the recent Turkish attacks. May God have mercy on us!"

At that moment, we heard sounds from outside the courtyard fence. Some young people were singing revolutionary songs. We listened.

"Hagop! Maybe these men belong to a revolutionary group and this is a warning!" My friend said.

With that in mind, we went back to our bedroom.

***

I was feeling relieved that I had settled all of my responsibilities with the college. At this point, only God could have paved the best route. That morning, I shared some of my worries with my classmate Georgi Tashjian. I felt comfortable to tell him my secret and we decided to go to the city and secure a spot for me on a horse carriage to Aleppo.

It was easy to decide on the caravanner. He was an Armenian from Kilis. He was a broad-shouldered man with a pleasant face. Early the next morning, I would wait with my bag and blanket on the road to Aleppo, not far from the college. He would drive me to Aleppo for one and a half silver coins.

That night, I tossed and turned with nightmares. The next

morning, with the help of my friend, I gathered my belongings and hugged him goodbye. Unfortunately, after the Genocide, I learned that he was deported to the desert with other students and died there.

The weather was murky as I waited for the caravan. It arrived and navigated us through the hills, full of gardens and pistachio trees. There were three Turks in the carriage who were headed to Aleppo for business.

Two soldiers on horseback unexpectedly approached us from behind. I thought they might be following me so I cautiously hid. They were looking for some soldiers' wives. Once they left, the driver, who had noticed me hide, asked, "Why did you hide, young man? Are you evading something? My suspicions grew when I noticed that you were leaving college. You can trust me, young man. I'm also an Armenian!"

"There were circumstances that caused me leave quickly. I have arrangements to make before enlisting in the army,"

I told him.

The man didn't ask further questions. Maybe he understood that I was running from the draft. Anyway, we reached Kilis that evening and the carriage took me to the Protestant church where the school was. One of my compatriots from Urfa, Mr. Garabed Keverian, who had graduated from college a year ago, was teaching at the Armenian Protestant School of Kilis. He was surprised to see me.

"Hagop, there are still three months before the end of the academic year. I hope you didn't leave because you were unable to finish. Please, come in. It's somewhat humid here but you won't be cold."

Without further conversation, we entered. I told him what had actually happened and about my arrangement with the college president. I told him that my return home was necessary given the worsening political situation and he agreed. He too was concerned about the looming political chaos and Armenians being massacred.

"I don't know much about Musa Dagh," he said. "If there are massacres on their way, how will the people of the mountainous Musa Dagh resist?" he kept asking.

A week before I left Aintab, I received a letter from Yesayi Yacoubian, a relative from Yoghunoluk . It was thoughtful of him to include a saying from his dialect which meant, "Turn your face towards us, not away." These words were on my mind for the next couple of days. Sooner or later, a disaster was inevitable. At the same time, as people of the mountain, we would not easily obey the Turks.

"There are no valid reasons to start worrying about a disaster," my compatriot comforted me. "If disaster approaches, I will defend myself against death," he told me, showing a Browning gun from his closet.

"Don't be so sure, my dear," I told him. "Everything happening around us shows that, this time, the Turks will not leave anyone alive. That gun will not assist you in any way. If your circumstances allow, come with me to the mountain."

We talked about everything late into the night. Suddenly, we heard a knock on the door. It was the caravanner from Kilis who was going to take us to Aleppo in the morning.

"Listen, son, I am unable to take you to Aleppo. The military authorities will capture our horses to use them on the front of

Palestine. I understand quite well why you, as a Musa Daghian, want to make it to Aleppo in these difficult days. Don't try. Instead, head to Antioch and continue the road to your village, Yoghunoluk . Soon, a Turkish caravan will arrive and you can safely go to Antioch. With God's help, you will reach your destination. When you reach there, notify me by mail and I will pay the travel fee of one silver coin. I know why you're going to Aleppo. I think you want to go to your birthplace so that you will be with your loved ones when disaster strikes."

I was forced to accept the caravanner's advice. My compatriot from Urfa also thought it was the right decision. I realized it was already midnight. I felt the end of my travel was near and soon I would have to face a battle of life or death on the mountain of Musa Dagh. Again, I advised my friend to leave the school and Kilis and come with me.

After sleeping for a couple of hours, the Turkish caravanner woke me up at four in the morning. There were three Turkish soldiers in the chariot on a special mission to Iskenderun, which had been recently bombarded by warships.

In the evening, we reached the inn, Kirik Khan, which was also a channel for multiple roads. It was cloudy and drizzling. It was on a long street lined with little houses. This place had witnessed the Adana massacre of 1909, as a result of which hundreds of Armenians were killed and their houses burnt. We entered the inn's courtyard where there were many other caravans.

That night, I had to stay in a room with the other passengers so that we could continue on our way in the morning. Our room was large and had a horrible heater at the center that emitted more smoke than heat. The topic of conversation was the bombardment of the city of Iskenderun by the British navy, which greatly interested the three Turkish soldiers from our caravan. I wasn't included in the discussion because they thought I was too young and immature to understand. I finally fell asleep in a rigid armchair for a few hours.

The following morning, I was freed from the presence of the Turkish soldiers as they left to Iskenderun on another chariot. I prepared for my journey to Antioch.

***

At noon, we crossed the old Roman bridge over the Orontes River. It was raining heavily. At the end of the bridge, the guards used to question passengers coming from abroad. Fortunately, they stayed in their guardhouse this time. Finally, we reached the inn, Kuchuk Osman Khan.

Kuchuk Osman had maternal Arab origins and spoke fluent Turkish. He was familiar with the people of Kesab and Musa Dagh. It was rumored that he had helped some of the Armenians of Antioch during the Adana massacre in 1909. He was a short man. He had some rooms available at his inn. Last September, when I was leaving for college, I had spent a night in one of those rooms. I went upstairs, to rent a place and he saw me.

"Why did you leave school so early, son?" he asked. "Where are the boys who left with you?"

I answered, "Some circumstances with my family obliged me to discontinue my education. They need me with them. Osman Effendi, I am from the village of Yoghunoluk and I want to rejoin my family. Are there any boys from our village here?"

I'm not sure he believed my explanation but he replied, "Indeed, I will do my best to find someone from your village. Your uncle, Boghos Agha, was here two weeks ago."

I went to my small room and fell asleep since I was very tired, leaving the rest to God. I woke up to Osman Effendi saying, "Wake up Yacoub Effendi, there's someone from your village!"

It was my paternal uncle's wife's relative, Gabayd Atamian. He was also surprised that I had left college early but I found a way to avoid his questioning.

To Musa Dagh

The six villages of Musa Dagh were about 20 miles away, situated on the shores of the Mediterranean Sea. Each village had muleteers who traveled to Antioch daily, except on Sundays, to fulfill various orders and buy grains. They also provided pack animals for passersby. Therefore, there were two ways of getting to the village. The first was to wait for the muleteers later the next day and the other, which would take six hours, was to leave on foot early in the morning.

Gabayd was eager to leave as early as possible so we chose to go by foot. It rained all night and then we headed out as the sun barely rose from behind Mount Silpius. Which madmen would go out in those conditions? It was still raining heavily when we passed the guardhouse and headed to the west.

There was an overflowing stream ahead of us and there was a small stone bridge built atop it for crossing. However, the water had redirected away from its natural course. During summer, the torrent would evaporate and people would be able to pass on foot. As we reached it, we noticed that it had become a whirlpool and crossing it would be very difficult. We had no other choice. Knee-deep in rocky water, we crossed with the help of others heading to Suetia. We continued our journey.

It was still raining and I was walking barefoot in the mud. After four hours, we reached the Karachay River, that flowed from south to north to join the Orontes River. If it had been possible to cross to the other side, our journey to Yoghunoluk would have been shorter. But, it was impossible and we were obliged to head towards Haji Habibli and then to Bitias over a bridge on the narrow valley. After another hour, we were able to pass to the other side of the Karachay through a bridge. I let out a sigh of relief as we finally reached a place inhabited by Armenians and were free from danger.

The rain had finally stopped. I rested on the hill and took in the lovely smell of the spring flowers. Spring in Musa Dagh was lovely after heavy rain. These fields fortified my spirit for my motherland and gave me greater purpose. It was the Armenian environment that gave me this feeling. There were Armenians from there to the Mediterranean Sea and I felt safe. I was certain that my fellow Armenians wouldn't betray me because there were experiencing my same struggles.

There were a few miles left to reach our destination. We passed from Southern Haji Habibli to Soutmou, where my uncle's farm was located. I changed out of my wet clothes there and we continued on our journey.

***

After six hours of walking, we reached the houses at the edge of my village. We were surrounded by the villagers and I spotted our relative Yesayi Yacoubian. He also questioned my early departure from college.

"What news do you have from the other side of the world?" he asked me. "We are isolated here. You read and understood my letter, right? I am happy that you came. I'm afraid there'll be a disaster against the Armenians again. Do you know that there are signs that we could be deported? I will discuss this with you alone. I shall repeat myself, I'm very happy that you came. What is education worth if our lives are at risk?"

I reached my home and everyone was happy. Although my grandfather welcomed me, he was worried that the Turkish authorities would eventually find me. I felt confident that I had obscured my tracks. It wasn't until 1919, when I was in Aleppo, that Mr. Vanis Nikolay informed me that I was being followed.

After one or two days, on a Saturday morning, Yesayi visited and invited me to go on a trip. We went to Gellir Hill and enjoyed the nature.

"Hagop, now that we're alone, tell me what's happening outside this place," he said. "What will we Armenians do when the rumors of deportations turn out to be true? We have many villages here on the hills and some armor to defend ourselves. I'm sure that we will also be deported towards uncertain destinations to die."

"There are no such rumors in Aintab that I'm aware of, my dear, our school was far from the city. However, the caravanner who brought me to Kilis warned us of an upcoming disaster for the Armenian people. Also, he didn't take me to Aleppo because he was afraid of his horses being seized on the road. In my humble opinion, we should organize ourselves, before it becomes too late. Do we have the necessary weapons to defend ourselves?"

"That is a very important question. After the massacre of Cilicia, people started to prepare. I'm not talking about simple hunting guns, there are some formidable weapons too. I remember your uncle bought a Greek Gras weapon. Go and request it, as you're the son of the Abadjian family. I'll arrange for us to go to the monastery ruins on the hills so we can practice shooting," Yesayi replied.

Living in Musa Dagh in 1915

It was April. The villagers were busy with sericulture. I noticed the village was filling with military runaways day by day. There were disagreements about the truth behind the deportation rumors.

In 1914, I had visited the Armenian Revolutionary Federation's club in Urfa, although I hadn't officially registered as a member. Haroutioun Der Khorenian from the American "Central Turkey" College in Aintab had somewhat forecasted the coming disaster in his lectures there. Sadly, he also later became a victim of the Genocide.

In Musa Dagh, I had many friends who were members of the Armenian Revolutionary Federation and many others who were a part of the restructured Social Democrat Hunchakian Party, such as Bedros Doumlakian and Yesayi Yacoubian. I became friends with Movses Der Kalousdian, Setrag Boursalian, Shefik Doumlakian from Yoghunoluk, Serop Sherbetjian from Khodr Bey, and others. I didn't have any organizational responsibilities, but the ideals of the Armenian Revolutionary Federation had been shaping my mind for years. I vowed to work for anything that would serve the Armenian people. As a result of my involvement, I grew very close to my Armenian Revolutionary Federation friends. Often, we would get newsletters informing us about the current situation and upcoming plans.

I visited Yesayi one night. He was sitting on the floor with a lamp and reading a letter from his brother Hagop who was in the United States. His brother had written that he intended to buy a ship and come to Musa Dagh.

"Look, Hagop!" he said. "Maybe the Americans are not aware of what is happening in the Near East. Are they not aware of our dire situation here? Let us see when my brother sets sail and where he reaches. If you want, we can go to the monastery ruins tomorrow morning to practice shooting."

The next morning, we went to the monastery ruins together. Even the villagers had no idea when or who had constructed that building. It looked like a monastery so everyone called it so. It had a rainwater reservoir that would also provide water for passersby. There was a steep hill with walnut trees next to it. It was perfect for shooting practice.

After giving me some pointers, Yesayi said, "I feel the time to use our guns will soon come and that's why we are practicing today."

We positioned a boulder 200 meters away. It was the first time in my life that I'd be using a military weapon. On my knees, I took a shot. I saw dust rise near the spot.

"Very good," Yesayi said, "you will be able to use this weapon very effectively against the enemy."

I felt as though I was in another world. We went back home

together. Nobody knew where we had been, not even my family. Yesayi was convinced that we would be using those weapons soon.

Day by day, the number of military escapees increased. I was introduced to many new people. One night, we went to Shefik Doumlakian's aunt's house to discuss what was going on. There, I was introduced to Bedros Doumlakian who had come from the United States. He was a short but handsome man. The topic of discussion was the impending deportations. We all agreed to resist the deportations and assessed our defense, listing our weapons and the men who had good practice with them. It wasn't feasible to keep the weapons with us. Instead, we would keep them in shelters and, whenever the need arose, go and get them.

We were expecting the unexpected at any moment. For this reason, many of the men would regularly hang around on the plains near the village entrance.

Part Four

The First Alarm

One evening, we were waiting for news from Antioch when the muleteers returned, informing us that they had seen Turkish troops practicing drills on their journey. Hearing this, we quickly gathered to plan and take action. Without hesitation, we decided to get our weapons from the shelters and head to the mountain. It was evident that the villages would be attacked in the early morning. We hadn't received any deportation notices so we assumed the Turkish authorities were coming to investigate our ability to resist.

Fifteen of us took our guns and spent the night on the rocky hills. In the morning, we heard shooting. The villages were attacked. The military authorities had come to detain some criminals and, as we had assumed, see how much power we had to resist. They searched for weapons and only found hunting guns. As they searched, they also stole property such as silk scarves and other belongings. We could see the villagers scattering in several directions, among them Tateos Kazanjian from Yoghunoluk who was shot near the rocky cliffs and died. We thought the army might think to check the mountain for the village youth so we decided to go farther up to Tataralang and Kuzjeghaz. We arrived there at noon.

We were on the hills of Tataralang when Hovhannes Kibourian, a man in his sixties, and the village chief, Hergelian, came to give us an update. The leading army officer had angrily yelled, "Where are your youth?" and threatened to arrest the priest and the village chief and move them to Antioch. The village chief had promised to investigate. We all agreed that they should return and tell the officer they hadn't seen us.

We moved to the ruins of the monastery and waited for more news. Shefik Doumlakian's aunt had brought us food and we relied on the well to satisfy our thirst. We were running out of our resources. On our way there, we had seen dogs roaming around the corpse of Tateos Kazanjian. A coffin was brought from the village and he was buried in the church cemetery.

We later learned that, to cover up suspicion, the army officer had confessed that the death of Kazanjian was an accident and decided to return to Antioch. Also, one of the lower-ranking army officers had decided to free the villagers they had arrested to deport to Suetia.

When we were informed that there were no more armed men in the village, we decided to return home in the dark. Setrag Boursalian was my neighbor so we made the trip together. When I was heading up the stairs to our house, I used a secret signal to let my family know of my arrival so they wouldn't get scared. My mother received the signal but my grandfather panicked, thinking the soldiers had returned. As I knocked on the door, he shouted to my mother, "Go and see what they are requesting! Give the bastards what they want so they will leave!"

"Don't worry Dad, it's Hagop," my mother comforted him.

As I entered, I saw the 80-year-old man sitting in front of the fireplace in deep thought. He was chain-smoking. Noticing my gun, he said, "The Bible says that he who uses a weapon will die by the weapon my son."

"The situation is very bad. They killed Tateos because he didn't have a gun! Don't worry, we will need this for defense someday," I answered.

"What are you saying? You think you'll be able to rival the Turkish army with the gun you are holding?" he asked.

My grandfather had witnessed how the Turkish authorities were undefeatable in previous massacres. He turned my mother, "Give him the necessary nutrition. Let him go! God forbid the Turkish authorities arrest him!"

This was our life in the village. Although there were no more armed Turkish men, we continued to keep watch and discuss plans. Sometimes, we guarded the village border through the night. Although we were sure that no villager would betray us, we spent the nights at the village's secluded houses.

Pastor Dikran Antreassian Returns to His Native Village

On July 12, 1915, Pastor Dikran Antreassian returned to his birthplace, Yoghunoluk, through Marash. We had a close relationship with the Pastor. I welcomed and greeted him and his wife. He was very worried about the deportations. Having been in Zeitun, he told us what had happened to the Armenians there, explaining how the brave men of Zeitun, who were once undefeatable, were also deported.

"I see there is a group of young men here who are ready to

resist the deportation order by all means. What is the current situation?" he asked me.

"According to your accounts, deportation implies death. Don't you think that it is much better to stay and fight for the land instead of dying somewhere in the deserts?" I asked.

"I saw a group of young men from Zeitun who went to the mountain, just like you are doing, to defend the land. But, when the majority of the villagers realized that deportations do not necessarily imply death, especially after the speeches of the Catholicos of Sis and Dr. Shepard of Aintab, they preferred to be deported and let fate decide their future. I couldn't advise anything and instead chose to return here, to my birthplace of Yoghunoluk, with the help of the American missionaries in Marash. Getting here was a miracle. Now that I am here, I have to reconsider the situation."

"It's evident that you don't have any idea of what is happening to Armenians, including the risk of annihilation. If our fate is death, isn't it better to stay and resist the unfair decisions on behalf of our people?" I replied.

"How are you going to resist?" he questioned me. "Do you have the necessary means? We, as villagers, are all good hunters. Our weapons are suitable for hunting purposes only."

"Your Honor, you know more than any of us about the recent state of affairs in Istanbul. The Turks will surely not tolerate our cultural advancements and nationalist will. We still vividly remember what had happened in Cilicia in 1909. Hundreds of people were killed in Antioch, including many people from Musa Dagh. We saw how the disaster reached our homes. We resisted by keeping ourselves armed and awake through the night. We saw how Antioch turned into chaos and took it as a sign to prepare by purchasing weaponry. This weaponry will soon be used in the villages of Yoghunoluk, Khodr Bey, and Vakef. What is your opinion on this? Should we be deported like Zeitun or should we fight for our lands and die with dignity?"

There was a moment of silence, after which the Pastor's wife, Araksi Antreassian, gave her opinion. "You have thought about this extensively and are giving your opinion based on your beliefs." She then said to her husband, "God, get this trouble away from us! We have reached our village safely but I can't think of how the situation will turn around. We are all descendants of our brave forefathers and are obliged to fight. As the psalm says: 'I will lift up mine eyes unto the hills, from whence cometh my help.'"

***

The next few weeks passed peacefully but my nights were full of nightmares. One afternoon, Yesayi invited me to his newly-designed garden, located in the valley of Saghtaras, where a series of hills divided it from the village. The weather cooled as the sun set. Yesayi's garden didn't have many trees so they had constructed a small pavilion for shade. When we arrived, a man was lying there half-asleep. He stood immediately as he saw us. He was Tovmas Aintabian, a military escapee from the village of Vakef. Tovmas Aintabian had traveled through the red mountain ranges and managed to reach Yesayi's garden on the road to Khodr Bey.

"I am very glad to see you," he told us. "I walked for 20 hours through areas inhabited by Turks. I am hungry and thirsty. I won't head to the village only to be arrested by Turkish authorities. Do you have any news from the village?"

We told him all the current information about the village, including that there was a chance of deportation. At night, we returned to Yoghunoluk and he headed to Khodr Bey.

There was a small stream on the road from where the water would flow to the valley. We were passing through bushes and blackberry shrubs when we saw a man trying to hide in the bushes. Yesayi suspected that he wasn't a fellow villager because a villager wouldn't have tried to hide.

He started towards the man who shouted, "Don't shoot, we are Armenians." We were surprised to hear them speak Armenian with an accent from Zeitun.

"You seem so familiar," Yesayi said to them. "How did you manage to reach here?"

These men were deportees of Zeitun who had gone through the deserts and reached the Orontes River, passing through areas inhabited by Turks. Since they were dressed like villagers from Musa Dagh, they hadn't attracted much attention.

"Listen, my brother, my friend is sleeping there, we're very tired. We are from Zeitun and are both ashamed that we chose to be deported with the others. We fled the caravan at night and have made it to this point by God's will."

We had to believe them. Also, the risk was low because Turkish authorities didn't trace Armenians on the move.

"Listen, my friends, the village of Yoghunoluk is behind this hill. We wish we could take you ourselves but we don't want the villagers to spot you. There is a cave behind this hill where we will come and get you," Yesayi told them. "My friend will bring you some food and water from the village. Even though you are safe here, and you are with Armenians, we advise you not to move from your place. You will soon be helping us in our battle against the Turks."

Then, he told me, "Go and send some food and water to the cave in the Koukairy valley, where these men will be staying."

I returned to the village while he took them to the cave. In the afternoon, before dark, I delivered food and water to them. They were happy to have arrived in an Armenian village. These men were kept hidden until everyone went up the mountain for battle. There, they fought extraordinarily.

In the meantime, many of us stayed at a house that was high up on the mountain. It belonged to a villager named Garmren Kevork. There was Krikor Nkrourian (nicknamed Yuzbash), Tovmas Aintabian, Movses Der Kalousdian from Yoghunoluk, Hagop Karageozian (nicknamed Ellion) from Vakef, Yesayi Yacoubian, Bedros Doumlakian, and many others. There were more than 40 of us there, meeting and discussing our dire circumstances around the clock.

One meeting in particular had a very important impact on the start of the battle. There were many opinions shared but I could not participate because I was on guard duty that evening. In the case of deportation, all the men agreed to resist even if it meant dying. Then, all we could do was wait to see how it took course. In the meantime, we delegated ourselves as guards around the villages.

Life Before the Resistance

In 1914, when a general draft was declared, Armenians were also included. All Ottoman citizens were required to fulfill their duty.

In his 1935 memoir, Der Haroutioun Toumayan, Antioch's priest, wrote,

"Suetia's mudir had orders to pursue those evading the draft, among which was a young brave man named Levon from Kaboussieh. One of the army officers tried to arrest Levon but to no avail. As a result, the head officer took his anger out on the villagers. Soldiers robbed houses, beat the elderly, and dragged people out to the streets."

Der Haroutioun informed the Catholicos of Sis and the governmental authorities but they were silent.

The men of Kesab and Suetia who were of military age registered themselves at the beginning of the draft and then returned to their villages. Some of those men actually accepted the draft and fought in the Turkish army. Others became fugitives.

On October 29 and November 5, the priests of Kesab and Suetia were told to advise the people to be more cautious and not spread senseless news, especially about the military activities of the Turks and Germans.

Der Boghos of Kesab, Reverend Koundakjian, and Der Abraham Der Kalousdian of Yoghunoluk (who was the surrogate for Suetia's archbishop), decided to cooperate with the government and urged people to obey the authorities and enlist in the military.

On November 12, 1914, the Catholicos was informed that

the issue in Kaboussieh had resolved and the mudir of Suetia expelled. He sent a subsidy of 50 gold coins to be distributed to the needy. However, the ghost of misery was ever-present. Governmental officials were suspicious of Armenian men, sharing reports of the Armenian men from Van who had rebelled, and so on. There was an order to collect all weapons from the Armenian men.

We received news of Zeitun surrendering and accepting the deportations. They had been deceived to leave their homeland and die in the deserts of Deir ez-Zor, even though a group of brave men had tried resisting. (For more on this, see Pastor Antreassian's book, "The Surrender of Zeitun.")

In March 1915, some Armenian soldiers returned home while others fled military service by going to Aleppo.

In the meantime, Der Haroutioun went to Aleppo on a special mission. He had planned to meet the wali and explain the difficult situation in Suetia, asking him to free the arrested Armenians who had been forced into the labor battalion for two months so they could return to the village and continue the necessary work that wasn't getting done.

This was how naïve people had become!

Although the wali empathized with Der Haroutioun, he was unable to help in any way because the authorities of Constantinople already had plans that they were going to implement. As the recent events had shown, this was sure to be a crooked plan. Unfortunately, some were too naïve to recognize and take action against it. The wali advised the Catholicos to go to Aleppo to find a solution. He also promised to send a letter to the responsible authorities but without giving much hope. Der Haroutioun returned to Antioch.

A member of the Young Turks was assigned as Suetia's new mudir. He was a deceitful man who only brought harm. With the aim of enlisting new soldiers, the new mudir went to Yoghunoluk. There, he ordered Toros, the son of Yacoub to be beaten to death. Also, in the village of Vakef, soldiers captured Vanes' wife and raped her for six hours behind a hill, and then left her to die in a pool of her own blood. These occurrences caused fears to rise again.

The Qaimaqam promised to look into the incidences, but his promise was in vain. The government was implementing what they had planned.

The community leaders advised Armenians to be very cautious and stay out of conflict. The priests and the mayors would try to convince the fugitives to surrender.

This was life before the resistance, as described in the memoirs of Der Haroutioun.

***

Finally, it arrived.

The people of Kesab received deportation orders. A meeting took place on July 28th, in Abraham Der Kalousdian's house, the priest of Yoghunoluk. Representatives from Bitias, Haji Habibli, Khodr Bey, and Vakef were also present. The representative of Kaboussieh was absent. The representatives of Bitias were Movses Renjilian, Kevork Sherbetjian, and Boghos Frankian. The representatives of Haji Habibli were priest Der Vartan Varteressian, Kevork Markarian, Haji Khacher Mardinian, and Hovsep Doudaklian. Der Abraham, Jabra Kazanjian, Movses Der Kalousdian, Bedros Kalousdian, Elias Masmanian, Bedros

Hergelian, Hagop Atamian, Boghos Kabaian, and Pastor Antreassian represented Yoghunoluk. Dikran Karajian, Melkon Kouyoumjian, and Yesayi Abrahamian represented Khodr Bey. Tovmas Aintabian and Hagop Karageozian represented Vakef.

The focus of this meeting was whether to follow the deportation orders or resist. Pastor Antreassian pointed out the tragic fate of the Zeitun deportees, the same people who once fought for their cause without surrender. The majority of the representatives considered rebellion the unwise choice, preferring to obey the authorities instead. Their position was based on our insufficient weaponry. Many opinions were presented for and against resistance but a final consensus couldn't be reached. The young men and military refugees decided to fight with everything they had.

Movses Der Kalousdian sent a letter to the people of Kesab, urgently calling on them to resist or send him their best weapons. Unfortunately, they did not join the resistance nor send their weapons. Perhaps some thought sending weapons to Musa Dagh was impossible, but it wouldn't have been difficult to take a small boat across the sea at night and reach the western side of Musa Dagh.

Why would we obey the deportation orders? The Adana massacres of 1909, perpetrated by the same authorities, were still fresh in all our minds. Obedience could only bring humiliation, suffering, and death. On the other hand, even if we died while resisting, at least we would die with dignity and on our land. Moreover, our mountain gave us a great advantage.

Some representatives at the meeting, in particular Der Vartan Varteressian and Kevork Markarian from Haji Habibli and

Movses Renjilian from Bitias, insisted on obeying the authorities. Also worth noting is Reverend Haroutioun Nokhoudian from Bitias who wasn't at the meeting but, along with Movses Renjilian, was instrumental in the people of Bitias accepting the deportation orders.

Notable attendees in favor of resisting were Jabra Kazanjian, Dikran Karajian, Avedis Masmanian, Tovmas Aintabian, and Hagop Karageozian. A few days later, Der Vartan Varteressian and Melkon Kouyoumjian also changed their minds and joined the rebellion. Finally, Pastor Antreassian, who was doubtful at first but later played a critical role in the battle.

The supporters of the rebellion thought leaving the coast of the Mediterranean was unwise because the possibility of being saved from the sea was high. They also hoped that the vile leader would die one day and they could return home. Thus, there was still hope for our people, though the panic caused nightmares and cynicism for some.

People worried about being stuck on the mountain through winter with little or no food. Some thought it was better to fight from the villages rather than the mountain. That was a ridiculous idea since the Turks would besiege them and destroy their houses with cannons. It was never seriously considered. It would be difficult for the enemy to conquer the mountain because it was at least 80 square miles. We probably didn't have the power to defend that large of an area, but we didn't need it anyway.

One thing was clear, we would fight and not let the opponent breach our boundaries. Maybe the enemy would eventually tire and divert its army to other places where they could be more worthwhile.

At the meeting, it was also discussed whether the Turkish

Aghas of Antioch would be able to save us if we sent representatives to try and bribe them. However, it was deemed a waste of time because those same Aghas hadn't been able to help during the massacres in Antioch. As long as the orders came from the central authority, the Aghas wouldn't have any influence.

Nevertheless, we sent representatives to Antioch in desperation. Many of those sent were from the villages of Haji Habibli and Bitias. When they were still in Antioch, on the 30th of July, official letters were sent to each village from the Qaimaqam of Antioch. On them, was a short introduction from the mudir of Suetia.

It's important to note that, just a short while before, the government had forced villagers to dig trenches on the hills facing the sea, probably in preparation for the arrival of soldiers there. Many villagers were forced to work tirelessly to dig the trenches. They even used pack animals from villagers without consent.

Some of the representatives sent to Antioch returned, while others were unable to. The ones who returned strongly advised the villagers to obey the authorities and deportation orders, believing that we would be led to a safety.

The Decree of Deportation

(The English language translation of this decree was obtained from Clark University's Digital Commons.)

Proclamation of Antioch's Kaimakam, concerning the deportation of villages:

Article 1- Considering that as from the date of my proclamation and within 7 days thereof the Armenians living in the kaza of Antioch must leave Antioch and the villages of the kaza of Antioch, each individual subject to this order must, within the above-mentioned, wind up his personal affairs and look for means of transportation.

Article 2- The police will ensure order and the well-being of Armenians, protecting them against any plunder while they will be dispatched towards localities designated by the government and during the travel.

Article 3- The government will supply the means of transportation and the food for the families whose poverty has been established.

Article 4- The furniture and the belongings that will be left here, will be inventoried one by one with their particulars and the government will put them into safe place and will protect them and the sums accruing from their sale will be put in the government's safe and as deposits and will be sent to them thereafter.

Article 5- All the rights of the deportees will be protected taking into account that they will be settled in safe localities whereto they will be sent.

Article 6- I have appointed a committee under my presidency to effect and direct the transportation, to protect the personal rights and to transcribe into registers the landed properties and the movables.

Article 7- All those subject to the deportation must have an absolute and spontaneous confidence in the government's operations and the other Ottoman subjects will respect and consider these rights which will be protected since the expedition which will be carried out will be an ordinary operation of emigration.

Article 8- I make it known that any person, be he from the public or one from the civil servants or one from the police who will have negligence in the execution of these orders will be immediately arrested and brought to court-martial.

The 16th of July, 331 = 1915

The Kaimakam of Antioch's kaza

Maarouf

To the Moukhtar and the government employees
 of the villages:

In transcribing here-above the copy of the proclamation in eight articles communicated by the Kaimakam on the 16th of July 331 = 1915 sub No732, I declare that you must prepare your affairs within the above-mentioned period of 7 days and be ready to emigrate.

The 17th of July 331 = 1915

The Maire of the Sueidia District

Khalid

The decree did not mention why Armenians had to leave their homes for the unknown. It only gave some reassurance that where they were being taken would be comfortable and so forth. But, these were empty promises and no one believed them.

Part Five

To the Mountain

What were we supposed to do? The Aghas in Antioch had still not given us an answer, but the people of Yoghunoluk, Khodr Bey, and Vakef had made their decision to resist. They started carrying their food and belongings to the mountain.

On the night of July 30th, we were faced with a decision. Two groups approached us from Antioch. The first group consisted of the fugitives that had escaped Aleppo. They had witnessed terrible atrocities and heard of even worse. They had heard of Armenians being killed on the road of deportation by Kurds and Turks, while their wives and daughters were taken captive by their killers. They insisted there was no reason to doubt the criminal nature of the Turks and no reason to remain passive. The second group was the Aghas returning from Antioch and unsuccessfully urging the people to obey the governmental decree and prepare themselves for deportation.

As previously stated, the Armenians had already made up their minds and decided to resist.

Did all the people who were climbing the mountain, children and old men alike, understand the gravity of the situation and the possibility of death? Maybe they did realize the glory of dying heroically. It was this spirit that encouraged future generations to shape their Armenian patriotism.

After 1915, we saw how the heroic battles of Musa Dagh and other villages became a source of inspiration for all Armenians. Half a century later, we should keep remembering those heroes and battles and recount them to future generations. It would be a shame to forget these heroic stories and not document them.

Having been on the hills of Musa Dagh myself, I witnessed how people were climbing without anyone leading them. I couldn't fully grasp the magnitude of what I was seeing. Why did all of these people listen to the advice of the few men who favored rebellion? How was it possible that we united as the people of Musa Dagh and chose to face death over the promise of deportation? How did all of these people ignore the threats of the Turkish authorities and the likelihood of death?

Let us acknowledge these brave and honorable people from these atrocious times and use their heroism as inspiration to always fight, rebel, and defend our cause.

***

After the 31st of July, countless men and women were climbing the mountain, carrying their supplies on their backs. The climbers of Yoghunoluk and Khodr Bey had to pass through tough pathways. On some parts of the mountain, there was no path at all. All men, young and old, carried their weapons on their shoulders. I saw some naïve people burying their pots in the gardens. Maybe they thought the horrid leader would be killed by the Allies and they would be returning home and retrieving their belongings.

Fortunately, it was not cloudy. People managed to reach the Tataralang plateau. The people were not well-prepared. Some had not been able to bring much of their belongings. People were cutting wood while climbing so they could build shelters. Only those who reached Kuzjeghaz had managed to stay in one group.

Surprisingly, this climb up the mountain wasn't stopped by any authorities, although some police officers kept roaming the villages. Maybe the government was sure that we were unarmed and could be herded away like sheep whenever they wanted.

On August 1, when we were still getting settled on the mountain, letters arrived from the mudir advising people to choose deportation for much better living conditions. He thought we would believe his pathetic promises.

On August 2, the inhabitants of Yoghunoluk, Khodr Bey, and Vakef had already settled in different areas of the mountain. Kaboussieh, with its two million inhabitants, had remained passive and only eight families had settled on the mountain. In Bitias and its neighboring Haji Habibli village, most people were still in the villages while others had started their journey up the mountain.

It was difficult to convince people to fight against the authorities they had been living under for a hundred years. Some searched for hideouts to wait out the turmoil, thinking of those who had managed to hide during the Hamidian massacres and had been rescued in the end

One of the men that tried to hide was Gabouyd from Yoghunoluk. who had helped me when I fled Antioch to come home. He hid with his wife and two children in a cave near the ruins of a church. The village people had kept many of their belongings there so some Alawi men knew about the cave. Two days later, an Alawi man entered the cave. Gabouyd grabbed his gun while his wife desperately tried to strangle their child to stop from crying. Gabouyd was forced to shoot and kill the man. After this incident, the family gathered their belongings and decided to join us on the mountain. It wasn't until years later that the child heard this story from his mother.

In summer, Musa Dagh was very foggy and humid. It was impossible to take shelter under the trees, as water would drip continuously. People knew there was no time to waste and immediately started building shelters for protection.

Some days later, a third letter arrived from the mudir, addressed to Der Abraham Der Kalousdian and Melkon Kouyoumjian, advising for the people to return home. The letter said,

"We heard, with great sorrow, that you both climbed the mountain with everyone. That was not a proper act, considering your dignity and position. You are clever enough to predict your fate the moment you are attacked by our forces. Therefore, I urge you and your people to return as soon as possible and surrender to the deportation orders of the government. Otherwise, you will be responsible for the massacre that will ensue."

The arrogance of these few lines was enough to reveal their true intentions. No one replied to the letter and people started to prepare for battle.

As the land permitted, the people had settled in four main areas of the mountain. The largest settlement was Damlajik because it was the closest to the sea. Each area would need an executive committee to prepare for defense. These four locations were: Damlajik, Kizilja, Kuzjeghaz and Kaplan Duzaghi.

Logically, the first step was to organize a defense plan. The leaders of Damlajik and Kizilja took on that responsibility for their headquarters, whereas all the men of Kuzjeghaz gathered in one place to discuss and listen to advice from Pastor Antreassian, Movses Der Kalousdian, and Movses Kabaian. After anonymous voting, seven men were elected, and three others were to be elected by the militants. As for Kaplan Duzaghi, they didn't take any action.

The mudir hadn't lost hopes of manipulating us. On August 5, he sent a fourth letter through a messenger for the priest of Haji Habibli, Der Vartan Varteressian, Haji Khacher Mardinian, Reverend Haroutioun Nokhoudian of the Protestant church from Bitlis, and Kevork Sherbetjian from Bitias. This letter was rejected just like the previous one. It was clear that the government wanted, by all means, to avoid an armed battle.

Reverend Haroutioun Nokhoudian was a Zeitun native. We all thought that he would be the first to head to the mountain for rebellion. But, he was a pessimistic and arrogant man, so much so that he didn't understand how the people of Musa Dagh had decided to die on the mountain rather than be deported to faraway deserts. We had met two years prior as we traveled from Antioch to Aintab together. We saw each other again in Tataralang. He was a witty man and I still remember what he said when he saw me, "Hagop, you look like a militant with that gun."

What was I to reply to a clergyman who was governing a community? I sensed the irony in his tone. "Go back down the mountain and send my regards to whoever sent you. Maybe you are more intelligent than us and we're in a state of delusion," I answered.

In his memoir, Pastor Antreassian wrote:

Reverend Nokhoudian wanted to meet me privately to share his opinions. "Pastor," he asked, "now that you have climbed the mountain, are you confident enough that you will be able to resist all threats?'

"Yes," I answered, "I hope so because I don't think that the Turks will be moving a large army this far when they are involved in critical battle elsewhere. Also, we aren't considered a threat to them. I know that the authorities can gather manpower from the neighboring villages but I think that we will be able to resist a troop of up to 3,000."

"I don't respect your decision and your unorganized system," he replied.

I explained that the unorganized system made sense given the circumstances.

He explained that the process was taking a long time and that the government would soon be sending letters and delegations to convince us otherwise. "If I see that the government has lost hope in convincing you, I will find a way to come. Otherwise, I don't have any hope for you."

This man thought that he would be able to climb the mountain at the very last moment. He was already very late. He returned to whoever sent him and joined the deportation with the others. It is still not clear how he was able to escape the deportation in the end.

In 1927, when I saw him in Beirut, I reminded him of the

pride all Armenians held for the people of Musa Dagh, the same people he once considered unruly.

"Who would guess that you would be rescued by the will of God?" he had replied.

The First Battle
Let us return to the mountain.

There were more important things to do than elect executive committee members, such as building barriers, dividing militants into groups, and so on.

On August 7, eight days after people had left their houses, representatives were called for a general meeting. The meeting was held on the Tataralang plateau. The participants were representatives from Kizilja, Kuzjeghaz, and Damlajik, and the newly elected representatives from Haji Habibli and Bitias. Reverend Nokhoudian and Movses Renjilian from Bitias were also invited. Hovhannes Kibourian, who had managed to escape Aleppo and join us, hoped that he would be able to convince them to join our rebellion, but they did not come.

Just after electing the chairperson and secretary, we were informed that around 200 soldiers from Yol Aghzi had come to attack. They had already climbed the mountain, thinking they would easily defeat us. The meeting was dismissed and we prepared for attack.

Twenty armed men from Tataralang were sent to the battlefield to join our guards. Some of the young men asked Pastor Antreassian, "Should we shoot the soldiers?" It was not easy to forgo the fear of Turkish authority even if it was the evil enemy. The men told him the only reason they asked was so they wouldn't waste bullets. We also sent word to the other campsites and they came to aid.

Upon seeing our fervor and organization, the enemy lost hope. Musa Dagh turned into a battlefield where armed men ran from one hill to another with smiles on their faces, shouting "Fight the enemy, don't let them desecrate us!" The flag of the rebellion had risen. True heroism manifested.

This first confrontation took five to six hours and ended with the Turks' defeat. The enemy was forced to retreat with five to six dead and some wounded. Mudir Khalid had been humiliated. He gathered his troops and went to the Turkish village of Kabakli to reorganize. We didn't have any injuries or deaths.

As the days passed, our troops reorganized themselves for better defense. They split into groups of 10 and reinforced the trenches and defense structures. It was necessary to surround the trenches with soil for defense, though some could not grasp how a bullet would not pass through soil. In places where there wasn't soil, boulders and thorny shrubs were placed in dense passageways for defense. These small acts showed the enemy that we were well-armed, well-organized, and ready to die fighting. Thus, they didn't want to grant us any more time to prepare.

The Second Battle

On August 10, just after sunrise, the Turkish authorities attacked for the second time. They attacked from the direction of Haji Habibli, from a site called Bakajak. The enemy first attacked the top of the Kuzjeghaz hill, thinking that was the location of our camp. Our 15 guards in that location were forced to retreat upon realizing there were more than 2000 fighters from the enemy. However, before the rest of us reached them to help, they had been able to keep the enemy from advancing. The troops tried to conquer us by taking advantage of the fog but the bullets fired by our brave men held them back.

I will call this conflict "The Battle of Omaren Gitayn."

Again, I quote Pastor Antreassian's memoir,

A day or two before the attack, the people of Bitias had decided to climb the mountain and join us.

The deportees from Bitias claimed the army had been 5000-6000 in number. The village chief of Bitias, Sarkis Sherbetjian, said he had hosted seven different army officials during those days.

Having heard this news, Movses Renjilian went to his relative Adaleh Mohammad's house on an island on the Orontes River. His relative informed him of the Turkish government's plan to exterminate Armenians and advised him to return to Bitias and convince the people to go up the mountain and join the rebellion. Movses Renjilian returned to Bitias by boat and didn't find it difficult to convince the people.

Also during that time, the Turkish army reached Haji Habibli. The head army officer called a meeting with the leaders of Bitias. Upon seeing the many troops and weaponry the Turkish army had come with, they all grew concerned. At this meeting, the Turks informed them that they planned to set the mountain on fire. A German officer that was with the troop said, "Isn't there a higher mountain? We will set our cannons at the top and bomb them until all natural beings die." The men were given the chance to convince the people to surrender.

After reading the memoirs of Pastor Antreassian, it is very

clear how the Turks and German officer were convinced they could destroy everything on the mountain and deport us like sheep. Though they did not succeed, we lost many men in this battle.

Eight families from Bitias had settled away from us with the hope of being rescued. The enemy discovered them and killed Giragos Kadian, his wife, and one other person, and took the remaining 50 as slaves.

In another place, an old man from Haji Habibli, Antreas Jouharian, and his wife were arrested. Kevork Falian, a tinsmith, was pierced by a sword but later recovered.

These events made it easier to convince the inhabitants of Bitias and the neighboring villages of Haji Habibli to climb the mountain and join the resistance, provided they had some leadership and weren't stopped by authorities before they had the chance.

It should be mentioned that Reverend Nokhoudian and Movses Renjilian caused 64 families to be deported.

It is also worth noting the three villages in the Yoghunoluk region. Of the three villages, only two families had not joined the resistance. In fact, the entire initiative for going up the mountain was because of these three villages.

The Battle of Omaren Gitayn

For defense, some others and I stayed in a huge trench on the slope of Kizilja. When the first cannon was discharged towards the hill of Evrenje, we heard a messenger calling, "The enemy is approaching from Bakajak towards Omaren Gitayn. Grab your weapons and go towards the hills overlooking Tataralang."

Going down the winding path, we reached a small plane near the plateau. We saw two Armenian men from Haji Habibli, their heads wrapped in white rags, holding a white handkerchief. It was clear they were trying to surrender to the Turks to save their lives. There was a brave young man from Vakef with us that ran ahead to warn them from doing anything foolish. When one of the men resisted, he tied him to a tree and said, "Son of a bitch! Do you think that the Turks will save your life when they see you have surrendered? If you keep insisting they will, I will kill you!" The man was terrified and complied. We untied him and took his weapon. Paradoxically, when we were finally freed and reached Egypt in September, that same man declared himself a hero.

We called this critical battle the Battle of Omaren Gitayn. The Omaren Gitayn field was located between Bakajak and Tataralang and surrounded by dense forest. There stood the slope of Evrenje with its paths to Kuzjeghaz. The narrow pathways were blocked with boulders and thorny shrubs to slow the enemy. The enemy aimlessly bombarded the bushes where the goats were feeding. When the fog would thin for a moment, they would fire at the goats.

Our men had formed a semicircle frontline that started from the hill of Evrenje and reached the western rocks of Tataralang. There were five to 10 militants at each headquarter and they were ordered to save their bullets and not use them aimlessly, although we were being confronted with thousands of bullets. Their cannon was unable to overpower our troops, who were strategically attacking from different positions on the mountain. It was so cloudy that it already felt like nighttime. It started pouring rain which caused the shooting to pause. Perhaps the Turks thought we were out of ammunition.

There was silence.

The enemy started again. Our men had intentionally abandoned their positions to climb to higher positions on the mountain. Thinking we had surrendered, the enemy began to attack again. It was raining heavily again. They attacked Tataralang from a 100 meter front. We had prepared trenches there in case the need arose. The enemy didn't realize that all of this was a war game and charged forward.

I was at the southern front. When we saw them approaching, we used a volley fire that killed many on the spot. Bedros Doumlakian was also shooting from his trench on the western front and pushed the army back. It is also important to note Bedros Galustian who, with just five shots, killed the four cannon-operators and rendered their killing machines useless. All our men were sharpshooters.

This battle went into midnight. The rain stopped again and the enemy finally grew quiet. We went down the hill to the valley and ate something. At dawn, the heavy rain picked up again. It was the spirit of Musa Dagh expressing its fierce anger.

Witnessing the death of his troops, the Turkish head officer had ordered them to stop the attack. The soldiers hid in panic. Our men didn't go after them to avoid potential traps. The next day, we discovered that the enemy had retreated, taking with them corpses and wounded soldiers.

The battle had ended.

From our army, Movses Atamian, Panos Feslian and Hagop Tavitian were injured. Hagop Karageozian, or Ellion, and

Boghos Andekian were martyred. When the young men were carrying the injured Hagop Karageozian, he had told them, "Please don't waste time on me. I'm already injured. Go and continue the fight." He was one of the pioneers who had led the people up the mountain. The villagers were terrified of him. He died before even reaching the campsite.

You could not imagine the chaos the heavy rain imposed that night. Wet soil was dripping from the roofs of the shelters and splattering everywhere. Women, children, and elderly were shivering from the cold.

After not eating for 24 hours, I made my way to the campsite in Kuzjeghaz with two men. We were unaware that the enemy had fled and thought we were going to be attacked again. We walked discreetly through narrow passages, wet and cold. We were lucky to avoid the wind. It rained incessantly and we walked for almost eight hours.

We got stuck in a muddy thorny pathway. Hovhannes, who was leading us, said "Damn you rain! I can't believe how we've gotten stuck here. I've taken this road many times and never been misled. I think we are close to the campsite. I'll fire my gun as a signal for help."

We replied, "Don't fire. That's too risky. Some of our guards may attack thinking we're the enemy."

Hovhannes didn't listen and fired anyway. After some time, a few of our young men found us and helped us return to the campsite.

The scene was awful at the camp. Mud was dripping from the shelters and all of our belongings were soiled. Grains, flour, and all kinds of goods were destroyed. It was a very dark night. We were overcome with hopelessness. At this point, did the enemy need to do anything else?

Fortunately, the sun rose the next day, filling us with hope and enthusiasm again. My paternal uncle built a fire and was drying out the wet clothes.

In a single day, August 10, the enemy had initiated an attack and withdrawn.

Part Six

The Organizational Structure

After the Battle of Omaren Gitayn, we learned from our mistake and realized it was impossible to lead from four different areas at the same time. Thus, we decided to have only one center that would send the necessary troops to the battlefront. Central Kizilja was vacated and joined Kuzjeghaz. On August 11, the inhabitants of Kuzjeghaz were also bombarded. We invited them to settle in the coastal areas since it provided many advantages for our defense. Consequently, Damlajik became the central campsite and also the main armed region. There, gunsmiths, shoemakers, and butchers occupied their corners. Militants arrived to rest while waiting for their next orders from the Executive Committee.

The Executive Committee was formed from the union of the smaller committees and was solely responsible for organizing and giving orders. The chairperson was Pastor Antreassian and the secretary was Mikayel Gegejian, who had also been a teacher at the school in Khodr Bey. Movses Der Kalousdian was assigned as the head of the army. He had two assistants, Serop Sherbetjian and Dikran Karajian. With 15 members, this committee had to plan, give orders to militants, and define punishments for those who evaded responsibility. They held meetings twice a day to ensure that the shelters and communication were functioning smoothly, and militants had sufficient footwear and nourishment.

Like this, a republican government came to fruition and functioned for 53 days.

All the militants were separated into 43 groups of ten. There were 400 men who were eligible to carry weapons and fight. Then, there were three Dynamic Groups, composed of 33 men in all. The Dynamic Groups would meet in the Tataralang plateau to make urgent decisions during battle. The leaders of the three Dynamic Groups were Yesayi Yacoubian, Bedros Doumlakian, and Bedros Doudaklian.

There were three groups of teenagers who were responsible for communicating with the trenches and delivering bullets. There was a group of women and girls responsible for providing food and water to the militants. Old men dug trenches, cut trees, and closed passageways with rocks. Finally, we had Armenian Amazon warriors, such as the wife of Boghos Kabayan, who fought beside her husband and stayed on the frontline.

It is also important to give a quick overview of our weaponry. We had 95 Greek Gras, two old Ottoman Martins, 11 Mausers, and 15 hunting guns with bullets. That was 123 useful weapons overall. Each weapon could take about 100 to 150 bullets, that we would fill and refill constantly. There were also more than 500 hunting guns that used bullets filled with gunpowder. For these, we had enough gunpowder to fill 30,000 bullets. Eighty-five percent of this was prepared and kept by the Armenian Revolutionary Federation Regional Committee.

This is all we had to defend ourselves. We became hopeless every time we had to face our lack of supplies and weapons. It was this dire reality that inspired Pastor Antreassian to think of writing a message for help on a huge white blanket and drawing a red cross on it to attract the attention of warrior ships.

***

Since Damlajik wasn't favorable for living, some families built shelters in Kaplan Duzaghi, which was 10 minutes away. Pastor Antreassian also moved there with some Protestant families.

I went to visit him one day. His wife was pregnant and feeling sick. The Reverend was very happy to see me.

"I am glad you came," he said with worry in his tone. "I have a plan. Maybe you can help me get motivated and accomplish it."

He handed me a paper with English writing.

"It is an amazing plan, Reverend!" I told him. "But which ship will answer our plea?"

"They say a man lost at sea will hold on to a snake to be rescued. Don't discount this idea, it may just be the thing that saves us."

He had already prepared two flags.

"I have already proposed this idea at our meeting," the Reverend continued. "They are onboard with it. We have even assigned two men to wave the flags on top of the coastal hill to attract the attention of the warrior ships. As far as I know, the coastal regions are under British control. Since you know English, you will lead the first group. We will send two armed men with you and you will give your Gras weapon to another militant. We don't know which ship will receive our message so we have also designated Khacher Doumanian, who knows French. He will lead the second group. A copy of the English message will be placed in a tin box so that someone can swim and deliver it to the warship.

A Plea to the Christian World
The paper read:

To any British, French, Italian, Russian, and American admirals, sailors, and authorities this petition may find, we appeal in the name of God and brotherhood, for the sake of Christ and Christianity.

Dear God, we the inhabitants of Yoghunoluk and six Armenian villages—about 6000 souls in all—have retreated to the region of Damlajik of Musa Dagh, that is a three to four hour journey west from Suetia, along the coast. There is no Turkish army between the sea and us.

We have settled here to escape the barbarianism of the Turks, the torture, massacres, and, most of all, the outrageous dishonoring of our women. God, I am sure that you are aware of the extermination plan that Turkey is implementing on our nation. Under the guise of deportation, Armenian Christians are forcefully evicted from their houses, gardens, and farms, from their belongings and wealth, and sent to unknown deserts. There, they are killed by barbarian Turks, Kurds, and Arabs. This plan has already been implemented in Zeitun and its 32 villages, in addition to Albustan, Geoksun, and Yarpouz. No single Armenian is left there.

At the same time, the people of Diyarbakir, Gurun, Adana,

Tarsus, Mersin, Dortyol, Hadjin, Kesab, Hasanbeyli, Aintab, Kilis, and others have been deported. And, the same policy is being extended to the 1.5 million Armenians in different parts of Turkey.

The man who has written this letter was the Protestant pastor of Zeitun and witnessed the violence that the Turkish authorities were practicing. It was painful to witness people like me deported under harsh such conditions, to see women, children, and elderly walking barefoot through the desert with no food or water. Along the road, one could hear curses and prayers. Under the pressure of great fear, some mothers gave birth to children in the bushes on the side of the road. Immediately after giving birth, they were forced by Turkish guards to continue the torturous journey to death.

Those strong enough to survive the hardships of the death marches were driven by whip to the southern plains. Some died of hunger. Others were robbed along the way. Others were stricken by malaria and had to be left by the roadside. And, as the final act of this evil, the Arabs and Turks massacred all the males and distributed the widows and girls among their tribes.

Some 40 days ago, the Turkish government informed us that our six villages must surrender to deportation as well. Rather than submit, we withdrew to this mountain. We now have little food left and the troops are besieging us. We have endured fierce battle. God has given us victories but the next time we shall have to withstand a much larger force.

Sir, we appeal to you in the name of Christ! We pray that you transport us to Cyprus or any other free land. Our people are not lazy. We will earn our bread if we have work.

If this is too much to grant, transport at least our women, elderly, and children, equip us with sufficient arms, ammunition, and food, and we will fight with all our might against the Turkish forces. Please, Sir, do not wait until it is too late!

On behalf of all the Christians here, your respectful servant,

Dikran Antreassian
August 20-September 2, 1915

The Rescue Flags

After a couple of days, both flags were ready. I was responsible for placing them on the hill overlooking the sea.

Meanwhile, two weeks had passed without any major conflict. Everyone thought the enemy was planning to keep us blockaded so we would die of starvation.

The Battle of the Assumption of the Virgin Mary

On August 19, on the Saturday morning of the Assumption of the Virgin Mary, the enemy attacked from four different positions. A vast army started forward on the road from Yoghunoluk to Yol Aghzi. It then divided into two. It was evident that the opponent didn't know where our headquarters were located, as it was firing in the direction of our shots.

The fog kept our location undiscernible. Our troops in Kizilja and Tataralang were able to resist the enemy, whereas our southern front was destroyed and our positions in Yol Aghzi, Kor Osman, and Lurch Zhayr defeated. No one was left in Kuzjeghaz and Kizilja since everyone had gone to Damlajik.

The enemy had a powerful force near the Turkish village of

Chanakli which came close to gaining territory. Fortunately, they got confused and lost in Tataralang since Musa Dagh was like a labyrinth. The enemy was moving with caution because of their previous defeats.

The Dynamic Groups were changing positions, reaching areas where help was needed. A big group was approaching from the east, led by two men from Kaboussieh who were captured in their villages and forced to guide the way. These men knew all the pathways to Damlajik. Fortunately, the Dynamic Group, who had our better weapons, had managed to kill the guides and soldiers.

Saturday was the first day of the battle.

I was on duty at the hill overlooking the Mediterranean Sea. We kept viewing the sea through our telescopes, hoping for the arrival of a rescue ship.

In the afternoon, the cannons were still firing at us. We were waiting for food and water. Losing hope, we hid the flags in the bushes and climbed down. The enemy had spent the night in the hills and had not tried to advance again.

We had 11 men dead and five injured. Jabra Khehoian, Krikor Nkrourian, Fend, Bedros Penenian, Baghdasar Mardigian, Sarkis Shanakian, Krikor Kibourian, and Hagop Kareyan sacrificed their lives. Misak Bayramian, Barsoum Khoshian, Hagop Havatian, Movses Hanessian, and Tovmas Kerneshian were injured. Sadly, the first three didn't survive their injuries.

The heroic loss of Jabra Khehoian and Fend is worth detailing. Jabra and Fend had resisted without losing hope. However, Jabra was shot and told the other men, "Please, do not waste time here with me, go and fight," just like Hagop Karageozian had done.

Fend had been a fearless militant but was cornered and killed. Some say that his hunting gun was sent to Suetia and shown to others as a gun that had killed five men before its owner was killed.

The injured men were sent to the headquarters to recover. Unfortunately, we had neither doctors nor medicine. Hovhannes Kibourian and Levon Kazanjian played the role of doctors since they had some idea of what to do. They used to wash the wound with water, then clean it with a special liquid, and finally wrap it with an ointment from Musa Dagh.

The next Sunday, when the liturgy was held, our lookouts alerted us. The enemy had crossed Tataralang with great difficulty and reached Kerteshints field, where there were defense structures. The opponents approaching from the south got stuck at the Karayr gorge, which was surrounded by dense forest. They weren't able to advance further. They were confronted by our attacks and retreated. In some parts, the battle had turned critical. A villager named Kernez had an old bomb that was thrown into the valley, causing a terrible blast.

Hearing the enemy on the other side of a boulder, one of our old but well-built men had tried to capture the enemy's weapon instead of shooting him. The enemy became terrified and left his gun to the old man and tried to escape. Instead, he was killed on his way back by our gunfire. Our soldier wasn't able to use that gun after all because it had a different shooting mechanism.

The enemy signaled their next attack by releasing a loud firing noise. Fortunately, having escaped from the Turkish army, our men understood the signal and prepared for resistance. All the Turkish soldiers who tried to climb the mountain were killed by Armenian soldiers and their bodies rolled down to the valley. Hundreds of corpses ended up in that valley.

We also started to sense death all around us. Some of our men grew hopeless and planned to surrender to save themselves. Fortunately, Manoug Kelejian caught them in the act and threatened to kill them if they committed such a dishonorable act.

On this second night of the battle, the hopelessness grew. The enemy was firing very close to the Damlajik headquarter. Some of the women, children, and elderly were running towards Kaplan Duzaghi to commit suicide in the valley so they wouldn't be killed by the Turks. Some barbarous men from Kaboussieh had informed the enemy of our location and it was clear that they had managed to find us.

That night, when chaos reigned, the militants of the Dynamic Groups made their last effort to attack the enemy. The fog helped them stay completely out of sight. The enemy's cannon fell silent because they killed the two cannon-operators. In just one hour, the surprise attack shocked the enemy and some of them turned on each other in confusion. Thus, the enemy's site was destroyed, leaving us an officer's sword, 10 Mausers, and around 10,000 bullets.

The news of the Turks' retreat spread. The panicked soldiers had fled to the forest and were killed by our men on the spot. Mules, pack animals bearing water, and meal plates were scattered all over the Tataralang plateau. Corpses were found near the well of Kerteshints field. On one corpse, we found a letter from the head officer, "To the leader of the third battalion, use all your means to conquer the southern and western hills. You should spend the night there. Food and water are available."

The leader of the third battalion had replied, "The forest is dense and the enemy's bullets deadly. Don't force us into complete destruction. I will wait for your command." Clearly, this reply hadn't reached the head officer because the soldier delivering it had died.

This was how the two-day battle of the Assumption of the Virgin Mary ended. Samuel Markarian, Samuel Boyajian and Kerian died, while Avedis Masmanian, Bedros Jelkian, Vanes Jelatian, and Hagop Khechounian (or Heblen) were injured. We didn't know what the enemy had lost then but later discovered they had almost 1,000 deaths and injuries.

***

Musa Dagh had been cleared of the enemy. The Turks hadn't discovered us. They had thought we would surrender and obey their deportation orders. There were no more attempts to attack. We had won, but were not yet liberated.

Their new plan was to stop attacking and blockade us so that we would starve to death. They used every means they could to stop us from getting help or food from outside. Nevertheless, the villagers of Musa Dagh knew the mountain very well and would manage to escape at night and bring back millet, corn, and other crops they had sown on their lands. It took a lot of effort from the enemy to keep the vast mountain besieged. From time to time, our men would plan random attacks to shock them.

Before this battle, some of our men had gone to Bitias and discovered Turks looting the village. They killed some of them and took a man named Mohammad captive. He was interrogated but to no avail. When asked how many attackers there were, he said there were nine armed groups.

"Mohammed, why don't you change your religion and be Christian?" our men asked him.

"To be an infidel?" he replied.

Upon receiving this answer, our men burst into a rage and killed him with rocks. Pastor Antreassian tried to stop them but did not succeed. Maybe it was for the better, as we wouldn't have been able to feed him. Unsurprisingly, this would have been the fate of any enemy in our hands.

My uncle had many fields of corn in Yoghunoluk and Haji Habibli. One night, we cautiously made our way to his field to harvest corn. There were some soldiers in a nearby farm. We could have attacked them but our priority was to harvest the food and get back to the mountain.

The next three weeks were relatively peaceful, although we knew that the enemy was not going to let it stay that way.

It was the end of August.

So what if our village houses were robbed? We had managed to survive, fight, and find shelter on this foggy mountain. Our last heroic battle had motivated us all, giving us renewed strength, hope, and the will to carry on. Deep inside, we knew freedom was around the corner.

Our lifestyle started to improve. There was even some trade. The Executive Committee acquired meat and divided it among the people. A list was kept so that everyone could pay for it after we returned to the village. Every Sunday, church ceremonies took place on the hill near our campsite.

Even amidst this positive turn, the Executive Committee could not forget about the looming dangers. The Turkish authorities would inevitably plan for revenge after having been defeated. We were aware that the enemy was rebuilding and preparing its armed forces. Therefore, our defense preparations were still critical.

Day by day, our supplies decreased and so did our hope. For two weeks, those of us assigned to the flags were regularly heading to the coast, hoping to find help. Some thought of building boats and waiting at sea to be closer but that plan didn't succeed.

All hope was on the flags. We were besieged. Even the Qaimaqam of Antioch had rearranged the distribution of goods in Suetia so that we would not have access. Our men had started to collect all our supplies in one place so that they could be distributed amongst the families.

We had learned a lot from this last battle. Our lack of defense structures was evident. The enemy was taking advantage of the dense forest and attacking from where we could not see. We took advantage of this time and rectified our mistakes. We built new defense structures and cut down the dense forest areas so we would see the enemy.

Again, I quote Pastor Antreassian's memoir,

We also learned that a more practical and effective approach should have been considered to maintain our soldiers' morale. A committee was created for this purpose. Its members were Yesayi Yacoubian, Bedros Doumlakian, Mardiros Jansezian, and Bedros Kalousdian. This responsibility was in addition to their existing military duties.

We were also advised to inform Armenians who lived abroad through the American Consulate of Aleppo. Thus, we sent three letters, one to the consul and the other to the Armenian Prelacy of Aleppo. I wrote the first one in English, Movses Der Kalousdian wrote the second one, and the writer for Boghos Pasha was likely Der Vartan Varteressian. We pleaded for the consul to deliver all important information to whoever necessary and to share it with others.

The letters were going to be delivered by Khacher Azabian, who was on leave from the Turkish army and had permission to travel. Azabian promised to take responsibility but returned the letters after a short while. So we decided to send them through the Greeks of Suetia. We never knew whether they were delivered, but we certainly knew that nothing came of them.

Pages from the Book of my Life

Part Seven

Who Was the Messenger of Musa Dagh?

A few years prior to writing this memoir, A. Apelian, a doctor from Kesab, wrote an article in "Hayrenik," the Armenian newspaper published in Boston. It was titled "Who Was the Messenger of Musa Dagh?" He noted the name of an Arabic-speaking Armenian man from Aleppo, who was the messenger for delivering our appeal to the consulate or whoever we needed.

In 1920, when I was in Aleppo, I had a conversation with Vanis Nikolay from Yoghunoluk. He said to me, "You know, Hagop, when I heard about the battle on the mountain, without consulting anyone, I decided to take the responsibility myself and go and ask for help from the American consulate."

***

As noted before, Musa Dagh had an executive committee composed of Jabra Kazanjian, Mikayel Gegejian, Krikor Tovmasian, Melkon Kouyoumjian, Tovmas Aghayan, Hovhannes Kibourian, Boghos Kabaian, Dikran Antreassian and Dikran

Karajian. Pastor Antreassian had moved to Kaplan Duzaghi with his wife after the latest attack. He was the chairperson of Damlajik's executive committee and used to visit Damlajik every day.

Kaplan Duzaghi also had its own executive committee that consisted of Hetoum Filian, Hagop Keshishian, and Sahag Andekian. The military supervisor was Hapet Iskenderian.

Kuzjeghaz's executive committee consisted of Hagop Atamian, Simon Shammasian, Hovnan Iskenderian, and Krikor Kelemian. Movses Der Kalousdian, who had previously served in Damlajik, had moved to Kuzjeghaz and was on this committee as well.

We were, of course, aware of how critical our situation was. Even though the attacks had ceased for the moment, so had our access to food and water.

Some, like Movses Kerekian, said, "I can't understand the benefit of waving flags with our hands. Let us build a ship and sail to Cyprus." They didn't have any idea how far Cyprus was. In another instance, we promised a large sum of money to an Alawi sailor to transport some families to Cyprus but he had refused. Ideas like these were unrealistic. The Turkish government was keeping a close watch on the Orontes River.

Help from the Sea

During the last days of August, we saw a warrior ship that continued its path without noticing our flags. But, that meant there was hope.

It was a Sunday on the 4th of September, the 45th day of Musa Dagh's resistance. We call that day the "Big Day" that help was finally granted. It was afternoon. We switched shifts with the French-speaking flag group. We had barely made it 100 meters when we heard a call,

"The ship has arrived; the ship has arrived." This was the best news that we could ever hear. A ship had reached the coast of Damlajik, filling our hearts with great enthusiasm.

An armed man was guarding our coast. The sailors had seen our flags and had approached them to read the message. My friends and I turned and went back up the mountain and saw the ship. "They have the French flag," I told them. "It will be good to have Khacher Doumanian there."

The name of the navy ship was Guishe. By the time we had reached the coast, Khacher Doumanian had already approached them on a small boat and met Admiral Dartige du Fournet, to explain our situation. The Admiral promised to inform us of a plan for aid within the next eight days.

Bedros Doumlakian, who also knew French, told them that the Kaboussieh church had been turned into a weapons' storage by the Turks. Two hours after reaching the coast, the warship bombarded the church, destroying all the weapons.

I began to head towards Damlajik with a friend. We only took a few steps when we saw Pastor Antreassian arriving at the coast.

"Who went to meet the warship?" he asked.

"Bedros Doumlakian," I answered.

"Wait a few moments, I want to see Doumlakian," he replied.

The warship came to shore and Doumlakian got out.

As we approached, the warship came closer to shore and lowered a raft in order for Doumlakian to return. At that moment, gunfire started from the cliffs in the north, aimed at the raft and the few of us on the shore. One of our men thought he should respond and turned to fire into the air. As I reached out my right arm to stop him, he fired. A bullet hit my right temple and I fell to the sand, lying numb atop the drifting waves.

I don't remember how long I was unconscious. When I opened my eyes, I saw a French sailor on the coast communicating with the warship and pointing towards the location of the Turkish fighters in the South. One of the sailors approached me and said, "This man is not dead. He only has a wound on his head." "Squeeze my hand," he said to me. He wanted to know whether the bullet had damaged my brain or not. Then, he commanded one of the men, "Take him to the raft."

The man who took me to the raft was Bedros Gharibian. "Bedros," I said. "Let us not walk together so that we won't attract attention." After some years, when I was talking with him, he told me, "That's when I knew your brain hadn't been damaged."

Bedros Gharibian took me to the raft and told me, "Go on, you survived! Let's see when our turn will arrive."

Bedros Doumlakian advised the sailor on the raft to immediately head towards the warship. We hadn't reached the warship yet when it discharged a mighty cannon in the direction of the gunfire and silenced the Turks. We could see rocks from the cliffside crumbling into the sea.

We reached the warship and I was climbing the stairs when I started to lose sight. I later woke up in a hospital bed.

This is how my life was saved by chance!

***

I was half-asleep, my head wrapped in bandages. I thought I was on one of the hills of Musa Dagh resisting the enemy. I heard moving vehicles which was out of the ordinary. When I opened my eyes, I noticed that a sailor was looking at me. He asked, "*Ca va mon enfant?*"

Although I understood some French, I didn't grasp what he was saying. I pointed my finger towards the water. The man brought me some milk but I couldn't drink it because my jaw was injured. He said, "You know that you have a severe wound and if you drink water you will lose blood. I came to check on you."

I can't remember how long I was weak. I heard the doctor say to the sailor, "If this young man manages to survive until tomorrow, I'll grant him 50 more years of life."

The next day, they took me to the surgical room and removed a small piece of the bone from my right temple, without anesthesia. It took almost half an hour and was excruciating. After the surgery, my suspicions were verified. My dangerous injury wasn't a results of the gun I had tried to stop but rather a bullet fired by the Turks.

I was lying in a hammock inside the warship so that I wouldn't feel the ship's movement. That morning, when I was looking at the coast, the sailor explained that the scene was Iskenderun. Like this, Guishe left while the people on the hill had to wait another eight days until news of a rescue plan arrived.

***

I thought the battle of Musa Dagh had finally ended but the enemy had attacked once more, thinking that we would be able to help the Allies and plan an attack against them. Their attempts failed, once again.

On September 7, the enemy conspired against us, realizing that there was no other way to defeat us. It was clear that they had lost hope of blockading us since we had already gotten into contact with the outer world. Also, the mountain could be useful for the French. Therefore, they had to stop our resistance as soon as possible.

On September 9, three Alawis approached with white flags and handed the guardsmen of Cheikh Yorde three letters. The first letter was addressed to Der Abraham Der Kalousdian and Der Vartan Varteressian. It read,

I inform you that we received good news from the Hama deportees. They reached their destination and are doing well. Why are you taking such drastic measures? The Ottoman Empire shall forgive you if you decide to be deported. Then, you can go and settle wherever you want. Your current actions will be the reason for your annihilation.

As you already know, 2,000 barbarous Arabs have besieged you from Haji Habibli and Yoghunoluk. If you don't surrender, you'll be massacred. I promise that this letter is the truth. It is up to you to decide your fate.

Benjamin Hekim

27 August, 1331-1915

Benjamin Hekim was a doctor practicing in Suetia who was used by the Turks to commit conspiracy. He was an ill-mannered and Turk-loving man.

The second letter was from Colonel Refaat.

(The English language translation of this letter was obtained from Clark University's Digital Commons.) The letter read,

To the Councils of the Moukhtars of the "vakfs" of Bitias, Haji Habibli, Yoghunoluk, and Khodr Bey:

Article 1- I recommend to you not to spill the blood of the aged men and the aged women, of the men and the women and of the children but to surrender.

Article 2- Those who will surrender must come, white flag in hand, to where my soldiers are.

Article 3- The young men and the men who wish it may surrender with their arms.

Article 4- Those who will surrender will suffer no harm whatsoever.

Article 5- In the contrary case you are responsible for the spilled blood. All the material and moral responsibility will be yours.

The Commander of the 131st Division

Colonel Refaat

The 26th of August 1331-1915

Attached to this was another note from Dr. Benjamin. *(The English language translation of this letter was obtained from Clark University's Digital Commons.)* It read,

If you will not answer within two hours, your chiefs, who do not understand, will be responsible for the blood of your children and your woman.

Give this letter immediately to Rev. Father Abraham or to Rev. Fath. Vartan or to an intelligent man. Oh! I beg you not to neglect.

Benjamin (Hekim)

The 27th of August 1331 = 1915

The three executive committees discussed these letters. Movses Der Kalousdian suggested not answering any of them. Hovhannes Kibourian suggested responding, "We are not fighters, but are faithful to your authority, as we have always been. We have withdrawn here so that we can live a normal life."

Pastor Antreassian strongly refused the foolish suggestion, explaining that we knew how deceitful the Turks were. "If they get such a reply from us, they will be encouraged to write back and make more false promises to deceive the people. We already have a lot of confused and scared men that would agree to obey the enemy. Such a response can only hurt us."

Pastor Antreassian suggested replying with a list of demands, in order to gain time for further deliberation. The Executive Committee decided to answer within 24 hours. This all turned out to be a waste of time because the enemy later attacked without waiting for our reply. The attack confirmed that letters were all lies.

In the meantime, Guishe returned to the coast and the Executive Committee informed them of the most recent happenings.

The Fourth and Final Battle

Five days before the start of this battle, the opponent used drums in the village of Levshiye, to invite Arabs from the deserts and agricultural laborers from Sheikh Marouf to Musa Dagh. The barbarous Turks had hopes of using those men to attack and destroy us.

Before the expected time, the Turks started their attack. At first, their troops advanced a lot but, we eventually held them back. We used the Mausers that we had won from the previous battle.

We knew very well that the Turks were playing games, thinking that we would listen to their advice and abandon the front of Yol Aghzi. If Turkey had some military expertise, they could have easily destroyed our troops. Nonetheless, they never expected such resistance and opposition from our side.

The confrontation was very fierce. Our bullets were very deadly this time. The Turks who were fighting as jihad were being shot one after the other. Since they weren't able to endure anymore, they fled down the mountain. We had only two martyrs and one injured.

In the evening, Doumlakian made his way to the warship and informed the sailors that the next day's attack would be on the warship. On the morning of September 10, the sailor who used to nurse me visited me. "They will all be bombarded," he told me, showing me the Turkish fronts.

And so, the two warships, Guishe and Deus Ex, started to bombard the Turkish barracks of Suetia and the village of Kaboussieh and Kabakli at nine in the morning. The people of Kabakli village were terrified. That place had served as the center for the Turkish officers. Now, Turkish women and girls were fleeing barefoot. Our armed men were able to see the movements of the crowd. The panicked people didn't know where to go. Our men on the mountain had received orders from the warship to guide them in the right direction with small flags. That day's attacks delivered quite a blow to the Turks.

***

Guishe finally gave us an answer.

The sea was under British control. The French government refused to grant us food or weapons, promising instead to take us to Egypt. Admiral Dartige du Fournet suggested for us to abandon the mountain. Our plea to stay on our lands didn't get anywhere. We were obliged to agree to leave since there was no hope of getting more supplies.

We all thought what a great opportunity it would have been if we continued our fight and successfully stopped the enemy from annihilating all Armenians. At a distance of 30 kilometers, it would have been very easy to destroy Antioch with two cannons.

Liberation

September 12, 1915 was the day of the liberation of Musa Dagh.

The people happily went down to the coast with their animals and belongings. Some left after kissing the soil while others prayed for the martyrs one last time. It was clear that the warships wouldn't be able to take everything because they didn't have the space.

Thousands gathered on the coast of Damlajik. Happy and sad emotions intermingled. People were sad to be leaving their lands, homes, and belongings. They could only take the things they could carry with them. Sewing machines and other property were burnt. Hundreds of animals were killed so they wouldn't be left to the Turks. The people were then transported to the ship using French rafts.

The warships that took us to Egypt were Guishe, Deus Ex, Amiral Charner, and Fotter. The transport started on September 12, eight days after Guishe had first approached us.

We owe all of our gratitude to the French sailors who were our saviors, saving our dignity and our lives. It is worth specifically thanking a few individuals. We thank French Naval Officer Diran Tekeyan who helped us tremendously. Also, we thank French Captain Brizon who was our guardian angel. Finally, we extend our greatest thanks to Admiral Dartige du Fournet.

Again, I reference Pastor Antreassian's memoir,

The Admiral visited us on September 8 from where he headed to Famagusta, Cyprus. He visited the commissioners of Egypt and Cyprus, asking them if they were able to accept us. The first answered "We don't have a place for them," while the second replied that they have already asked London about it. The first telegram sent to Paris had arrived late, on September 15, due to a mistake. However, the second telegram had been successfully transmitted on September 10 and the reply arrived on September 14. The reply asked, "Where is Musa Dagh?"

The Admiral was aware of the imminent danger we were in and so took on the responsibility of sheltering us himself before finding a stable location. He commanded his troops to take us in. After that, his position was transferred to Dardanelle. Through the efforts of his successor, Dario, and the French Ambassador of Egypt, Mr. Defrance, we were eventually welcomed to Egypt.

To Egypt

It took 24 hours until the warships anchored in Port Said. There should have been a witness to see how our men were handing their weapons to the sailors! Everyone was transported to the eastern coast of the Suez Canal and settled in tents that were prepared for them.

Years later, in the Damlajik camp of Musa Dagh, a monument with a cross was placed near the graves of our heroes. All my respect to their corpses! My mind travels to Musa Dagh and its foggy hills…

The martyrs of Musa Dagh were Hagop (Ellion) Karageozian, Boghos Andekian, Krikor (Yuzbash) Nkrourian, Hovhannes Koujanian, Baghdasar Mardigian, Kapriel Khehoian, Bedros Penenian, Sarkis Shanakian, Krikor Kibourian, Hagop Sevougian, Misak Bayramian, Barsoum Khoshian, Hagop Havatian, Samuel Boyajian, Samuel Markarian, Hapet Vanayan, Hovhannes Lourchian, and Bedros Havatian,

The wounded heroes of Musa Dagh were Movses Atamian, Hagop Tavitian, Tovmas Kerneshian, Yenovk Keosheyan, Avedis Sasmanian, Panos Feslian, Khacher Blloutian, Movses Hanessian, Boghos Jelkian, Vanes Jelatian, and Hagop Abadjian.

Part Eight

The Armenians of Port Said

The city of Port Said was located at the entrance of the Suez Canal and had two factions. Most of it was European with modern buildings and business, while the smaller western region was inhabited by Arabs.

The preexisting Armenians of Port Said were very few. I got into contact with the Kalfayans, of which I remember Miss Rose Kalfayan who provided enormous aid to the camp inhabitants. There was an old man, Gapriel Tekeyan, who had a small kiosk where he sold cigarettes. Many of the camp inhabitants would visit him asking for aid. Although he was not literate, he had been raised with nationalist ideals. The president of the British and Foreign Bible Society was an Armenian named Aram Atanassian, who later became the godfather at my wedding.

On the Eastern coast of the canal lived Comrade Adom Takvorian and Azar Temizian from Urfa. It was because of Comrade Adom Takvorian's initiative that a coastal Armenian Revolutionary Federation group was organized and operated for a couple of years. In 1922, Comrade Adom Takvorian informed us of an upcoming visit from the Prime Minister of Armenia and other government officials. He invited us to welcome them at the custom house.

The group consisted of the Prime Minister of Armenia, Hovhannes Kachaznouni, Simon Vratsian and his wife, Levon Shant, and Hovhannes Devejian. Comrade Hrachya had come from Alexandria. We had the honor of hosting Kachaznouni, Vratsian, Levon Shant, and Devejian for a couple of hours, after which they headed to Alexandria.

I quote Mr. Nshan Tokatlian, an Armenian who was an inhabitant of Port Said,

News of the arrival of Armenians in Port Said had spread through Cairo. Every Armenian talked about the 4000 Armenians settling in Port Said. How could one remain passive against this wonderful news? They were the sole survivors of the Turkish barbarism and I was eager to know their origins.

That night, the political assembly of Cairo requested for me to visit Port Said with G. Kechian and M. Prudian. My responsibility was to stay in the refugee camps for nine months as a translator, representing the prelacy.

On September 14, 1915, A French soldier had brought some of the refugees to a place called Lazareth near the Asian border, which was located on the Asian coast of the canal. That place once served as a quarantine for those on a pilgrimage to Mecca. There, the Egyptian health department owned a hospital and buildings for the physicians and employees to live in.

On September 15, the second boat of refugees arrived at the port, packed with people. As we greeted them, they became joyful in realizing we were fellow Armenians. We asked about their situation and how they had managed to reach here. We couldn't understand their dialect and asked them whether there were any Armenian speakers. "We don't know Classical Armenian," they said. They sought out a young man who understood how we spoke and we communicated through him.

At the entrance of the canal, many camps were already prepared while the rest were under their way. The French sailors gave the refugees soup, meat, cheese, and some bread.

Life at the Camp

As soon as the ship anchored, the injured men were sent to the hospital for treatment. We were five in total in the hospital room. The humble wife of the British military leader of Port Said, Mrs. Elgood, used to visit us every day. We were also visited by Miss Rose Batmanian and Miss Aznive Berberian from the Armenian Red Cross Society.

One day, Tovmas Kerneshian said to me, "You studied English in college! Why don't you communicate with them and ask for more nutritious food? Our wounds won't heal if we keep eating low-fat cheese." That afternoon, when the woman visited, I said to her in English, "Mrs. Elgood, is it possible for us to receive more nutritious food?"

"Wonderful," she said. "Where have you learned English? Yes, I will discuss your request with the Arab provider."

The next day, we received more nutritious food. In the meantime, Mrs. Elgood informed the camp's military leader that one of the injured refugees knew English. As for my wound, Dr. Arsharouni promised that I would be healed in one month.

After a couple of days, they gave me the responsibility of answering phone calls in the administrative office of the camp.

It was not a difficult job but, since I didn't know Arabic, I wasn't much help.

Major Pearson was in charge of managing the tent distribution. After considering all the factors, he granted each village 25 tents.

It was not easy to organize this place in such little time. Anyone watching from the outside would see that the camp was very active. Children used to play on the narrow passages between the tents. The elderly sat in front of their tents dreaming of their past lands.

After setting up the tents, it was time coordinate food. For 10 days, people ate only cheese, bread, and olives, until a kitchen was constructed. The number of people in each family and their ages were recorded to distribute food accordingly. The count was a total of 4058 people, consisting of 427 children age 4 and younger, 508 girls ages 4 to 11, 628 boys ages 4 to 14, 1441 women age 14 and above, and 1054 men age 14 and above.

After that, the people were vaccinated. Mrs. Elgood led the process together with three Armenian doctors—Arsharouni, Churukian, and Deovletian— and three nurses from the Armenian Red Cross Society—Sirakian, Batmanian, and Berberian.

The People of Musa Dagh

In his memoir, Pastor Antreassian described the refugees that had settled in Port Said,

Who are they? How many of them are there? What is their history? Before the heroic resistance of Musa Dagh, the Armenian community didn't know anything about them. They weren't even aware of their existence. This was the first they had heard of Armenians from Suetia.

However, once learning about them, Armenians became very proud of the refugees' heroic resistance. Their story was repeated over and over. Even foreigners heard about the resistance and bravery of the fighters. An American newspaper had written, "The resistance of Suetia can be considered the most interesting part of World War I."

The people of Musa Dagh were villagers. Twenty-five kilometers from Western Antioch, there was a chain of Armenian villages, spreading from Musa Dagh and reaching the coast of the Mediterranean Sea.

The first link in the chain was Bitias, notable for its wells. The Karachay, a river streaming from the Orontes River, flowed beneath this village. According to legend, the German crusaders' Emperor Frederick Barbarossa had drowned in this river. The ruins of Saint Hovhan Voskeperan's home and monastery were located on the western side of this village. On the day of the Assumption of the Virgin Mary, many people would gather there to sing, dance, and play drums. Before the battle, this village was composed of 195 families, 1050 people in total. Of them, 113 families, with 423 females and 150 males over the age of 10, and 106 boys and 101 girls under the age of 10 were transported to Port Said. 450 of them served in the Turkish army. The rest obeyed the deportation orders.

Haji Habibli or, as the villagers called it, "Heblek," was located at the south of Bitias, separated by a steep valley. There were hills at its south and west. This was the only place one could see the end of the sea. It looked like a small city because the houses were built close to each other. The village also had a well. Before the battle, there were 257 families in the village,

1284 people in total. From this, 157 families were transported to Port Said, 900 in total. This consisted of 345 females and 267 males age 10 and above, and 153 boys and 135 girls age 10 and under. The remaining 384 either served in the Turkish army or were deported.

The village of Yoghunoluk was located to the west of Haji Habibli, a one hour walk away. The northern part of the village included part of Musa Dagh, where one could view the Mediterranean Sea and Jebel Aqra. This gave the impression that the village was 2000 feet above sea level. Yoghunoluk had three churches: Orthodox, Protestant, and Catholic. Before the battle, the village was inhabited by 255 families, with 1233 people in total. Fortunately, almost all of them, 1176, took part in the resistance and were transported to Port Said. Only two families and some old men, roughly 60 in total, chose to be deported.

Next, the village of Kaboussieh was located to the west of Yoghunoluk. Between these two villages, there was a village named Kabakli that was inhabited by Turks. This was the only Turkish village that had dared remain in the midst of the Armenian villages, like a thorn. Kaboussieh was located on the western part of Musa Dagh. It could be considered a Mediterranean region, as the sea was on its southern end. Its houses were built very close to each other and surrounded by gardens, where lay the ruins of ancient Seleucia. The people of Seleucia had once built a port that would welcome ships from the West. Alas, it was now far from the sea. To protect it from flooding, an underground passage was constructed on which the name "Vespasian" was engraved. Kaboussieh had only one Orthodox Church. Before the battle, 251 Armenian families lived there, 1125 people in all. The majority of them chose deportation. Only 17 families, consisting roughly of 22 females and 29 males age 10 and above, and 18 boys and girls under the age of 10, resisted. All in all, 85 people from Kaboussieh participated in the resistance and were transported to Port Said.

The village of Khodr Bey had two churches, one Catholic and the other Orthodox. There lived 195 Armenian families, 1149 people in all. Of this number, only one family and 60 others remained in Turkey for military service. The rest took part in the battle and were transported to Port Said. This totaled 1084 people, with 490 females and 326 males age 10 and older, and 136 males and 132 females younger than 10.

The village of Vakef was located half an hour away from Khodr Bey. It had only one Orthodox church. Before the battle, it was inhabited by 82 Armenian families, 470 people. Of these, 386 chose to resist and were transported to Port Said. That included 152 females and 114 males age 10 and older, and 61 boys and 59 girls younger than 10. Only three or four families and a few others preferred to be deported, with 84 remaining in Turkey.

Aside from these villages, there were smaller ones such as Veri, Nerke Ezzeir, Manjelak, and Kejdelak. Their numbers were combined and mentioned with the numbers of Khodr Bey.

Thankfully, Pastor Antreassian recorded this detailed information for the villages of Musa Dagh in his memoir.

***

It is also worthy to tell of the customs and educational system of the villages of Musa Dagh.

As mentioned before, the courageous people of Musa Dagh had decided to live on land where there were no flat areas. Therefore, they were obliged to meet their nutritional needs through the outside world. The only place they could reach was Antioch. Muleteers would go to the city daily for wheat and other essentials. There were also pawnbrokers in the villages that would help families get by.

The life of a villager was not easy. They could barely fulfill their daily needs. Their mountainous origins had given them strength and skills. They built things with their own hands, bred and sowed berries, olives, and figs. These three trees didn't need much water. In Khodr Bey and Vakef, they cultivated orange, lemon, peach, and loquat trees. The pine tree of Khodr Bey was famous. The people of Bitias cultivated corn and potatoes and even made charcoal on the hills. That income was enough to live on.

At the top of Musa Dagh, there were valleys and plateaus, such as Omaren Gitayn, Tataralang plateau, and Kertes⊠ints field, all of which became a battlefield during the resistance.

Each village had its herd of goats, which would graze on the lower hills and pathways. There were few carnivorous animals so meat was only available once a week. Some oxen were used to plow the fields. There was no milk delivery.

The main occupation of the villagers was sericulture, and this gave way for cultivating berries. As in other places, the villages had some rich lenders who would pay for the silkworm. If a sale was not successful, the whole family would be in debt, in addition to being deprived of necessities.

Fortunately, the people of Yoghunoluk would also work

as comb-makers, Bitias as spoon-makers, and Haji Habibli as basket-weavers. This way, they were able to buy their necessities. Some felt lucky if they were employed and paid weekly.

This was the economic situation before the beginning of the battle.

As for the educational system, the church in each village had a school where Turkish was taught in Armenian letters because it was compulsory. This was a result of Hamidian rule and, in part, the propaganda of Protestant missionaries.

However, after the implementation of the phony Ottoman Constitution, Armenian education had an opportunity to flourish. Nationalist songs were taught and political parties founded. The situation improved until the massacres of Cilicia brought darkness.

At the Armenian Refugee Camps of Port Said

In Port Said, people were able to go about their daily lives relatively normally. I was almost healed and thinking to find a job. I had two friends. One was Movses Khehoian, who had studied at an American college. His brother was martyred during the second battle on the mountain. My other friend was Nigoghos Nigoghossian, who had studied at an English college.

Before the start of the battle, Nigoghos had been visiting the village on leave. He ended up retreating to the mountain with us and was also transported to Port Said. One day, he approached me and said, "You know, the British are planning to register the men who speak Turkish and English as translators for Dardanelle. I already applied. Let's go to the camp office and meet Captain McFarland. Maybe he will register you and

Movses Khehoian too."

The Captain happily welcomed our applications and told us to prepare to leave for Cairo.

It was very difficult to leave my family. My mother cried. On October 9, 1915, when I left, I realized I was heading for the unknown. The three of us went to the refugee office of Port Said to meet Mr. Hornblower, who was going to advise us and assign our tasks. There, we met Mr. Gordon, a Jewish man, who took us to the train station. "Listen, a soldier will welcome you at the Cairo train station and lead you to the head office of the army," he said to us and left.

We reached the Cairo train station after three hours. The soldier that greeted us was Egyptian and spoke Arabic, which only Nigoghos could understand. He sent us to the army office where we met Pastor Megdichian, the official translator. The military officer tested our English language fluency and told the Pastor, "These men are newcomers to the city. Take them to an Armenian hostel."

Thus, we went to an Armenian hostel where we stayed for two days. Sarkis Hakisian from Musa Dagh visited us and took us sightseeing in the city. It was the first time that we had seen a city lit up at nighttime!

We went to the editorial office of "Housaper," accompanied by an Armenian Revolutionary Federation member. We met Suren Bartevian, who wrote an editorial on us the next day, titled "The Young Men." He used to imagine the Musa Dagh militants as huge middle-aged men and was astonished to see we were young men just like everyone else.

We also visited the Armenian Prelacy of Bein El-Sourein to

meet Bishop Torkom Koushagian. After we greeted his assistant, he told us, "Listen young men, you are going to unknown places where people may not know about Armenians. With all your effort, inform them and let them know how we are the sons of a tortured nation."

To Dardanelle

Preparations were made for us to set sail from Alexandria towards the Aegean Sea. At noon, we were already on one of the military transport boats as second class travelers.

The boat anchored in the Greek Port of Lemnos. We were sent to another Greek island, Imbros, located near the Gallipoli Peninsula. Nigoghossian wasn't able to continue with us from that point because he felt ill. He was to join us later.

In the afternoon, we were able to see the coast of the Gallipoli Peninsula. At times, we heard cannons firing. In the morning, we arrived at the southwestern coast of the peninsula using a small boat. A deputy was waiting for us. "Which one of you are Aram Touloumbajian and Hagop Abadjian?" he asked. When we stepped forward, he told us to follow him.

We had a military knapsack. After walking for half an hour, we reached a military storage from where we took two wool blankets and a tarp for our tent. We reached the 29th Headquarters of the army which was next to a hill. An officer who spoke poor Turkish gave us a pickaxe and said, laughing, "Unfortunately, we don't have a place for you to stay. We all spend the night in small pits we dug ourselves. Dig a small place for yourselves and cover it with your tarp." He left.

Life in Dardanelle

Early the next morning, one of the soldiers led us to a room that had a table and two chairs. There was a stack of papers on the table, most of them bloody. "Who can translate these papers from Ottoman Turkish to English?" he asked. "You don't have to pay attention to grammar." Although my friend Aram knew how to speak Turkish, French, and some English, he didn't know Ottoman Turkish.

"I know how to read and write Ottoman Turkish,"
I told him.

"So go and work on these papers in your cellar and bring them back as soon as you're done," he replied. I spent one day working on those dirty bloody papers. It was clear that the military authorities wanted to analyze the enemy's position and structure from those papers.

Other than that, there were no major assignments except for the interrogation of captives. This is what we did in Dardanelle. Fortunately, the kitchen was near and we were served tea often.

In the North, there was a road that led to the coast of Saros. Sometimes, an automated bicycle would go up this hill and, often, we would hear cannons firing from the faraway Turkish bases. We got used to hearing the bombs. One day, a bomb hit an Indian carrier who was leaving our base. It killed his horses and injured his legs.

Only one time, Aram and I requested special permission and crossed that road to visit an Armenian translator from Cilicia, Garabed, at his base on the coast of Saros. When we reached the site, a shrapnel bomb exploded 100 meters in front of us. One bullet hit my back without wounding me. I kept that bullet for a long time. Yes, our journey was a risk that only fools would take. Nonetheless, we returned safely.

This was how we lived. Although we wore military uniforms, we were not allowed to leave. Since the water was very scarce, we couldn't even shower.

It was the second week of November 1915.

Two days earlier, an interrogation of one captive had revealed that the enemy's trenches were behind the hills. We had the opportunity to watch what was going to happen in the faraway hills. At six, a missile was released. Then, the British navy and one Japanese warship started to bomb the Turkish locations for two hours. The scene was terrifying.

The next morning, the 29th Headquarters started its attacks. The Australian and New Zealand Army Corps conquered the trenches where hundreds were buried.

As a result, we had some captives, among them an army officer. He lied and said he was a plain soldier sent to Dardanelle from Aleppo but I revealed his position. He had been hiding in one of the trenches. Hearing this, our head officer shouted, "Who gave you permission to lie?" Then he told me to take him to the watchtower and have him show us the location of the Turkish troops.

A guard and I took him up to the watchtower blindfolded. The man said, "I was in the trench on the right. I went crawling and hid under the rocks. I was sure that you would find me after the bombardments. I'm happy that I escaped Turkish authority." We deciphered the name and number of his military unit from his uniform.

At first, I doubted what he was saying but, when he told us that he was from Antioch and specifically Suetia, I started to believe he was harmless, especially because I was familiar with the accent with which he spoke Turkish.

The captive's answers were being recorded by the guard who used to work in the British Embassy of Constantinople and knew how to speak some Turkish. I had once told him about the battle of Musa Dagh but he hadn't believed it was true, doubting the ability of such a small number of Armenians to resist.

I asked permission to ask a few questions about Musa Dagh in particular. The captive said that he had seen the Armenians fighting against the Turkish forces for 50 days and then they were transported far across the sea by French warships. This time, the guard heard the story of our heroic resistance from the captive's mouth.

During that period, many soldiers caught an intestinal illness and died, and rumor spread that the Dardanelle base would soon shut down. Who knew what covert political motives were at play? After about a week, Lord Kitchener visited and gave orders for discharging the base.

Discharging Dardanelle

It was the second week of January 1916. We arrived in Alexandria on a big boat. On January 20, our mission for the military had ended. Nobody knew why we had been told to abandon Dardanelle after it had cost 120 lives. The army paid for our stay at an Armenian hotel named Besdigian, for a week. We collected our wages, received a certificate, and were relieved of our duties.

My job in the military and interrogations of the captives had shown me how hopeless the Turks were. We were all expecting Constantinople to be conquered any day. One of the captives had said, "There is no real force in your way, why don't you take action?"

Returning to Port Said

In the first week of February, we went back to the Port Said camps by train. Having been gone for nearly five months, I noticed how the camp had transformed. There were now offices for the men and embroidery workshops for the women. The Armenian Red Cross Society had sent Armenian doctors and nurses to help the thousands of survivors.

I couldn't stay unemployed. I went to Cairo for a short time to join the British army but I returned to the camp to find a job close to my family instead. When I had been in Cairo, I had the chance to meet Mr. Trowbridge, the brother-in-law of the president of the American "Central Turkey" College in Aintab, Dr. Merrill. "It's unwise to stay here when you have all the means to continue your studies in the U.S. I can manage your travel expenses," he had said to me. It was a great opportunity but I didn't take advantage of it. My nationalist fervor and need to stay close to my family were more important to me.

Thus, I dedicated my life to the cultural liberation cause. With the help of Pastor Antreassian, we gathered a group of our friends and organized some lectures. My friends were Movses Der Kalousdian, Geghard Sharayan, and Serop Sherbetjian. The secretary of the camp, Mr. Mihran Siraganian, also joined us.

The camp had become a place of pilgrimage where many would visit. In April 1916, the editor of "Housaper" newspaper, Comrade Stephan Yesayan, arrived at the camp and distributed

1,000 American dollars. This money was from the Armenian Revolutionary Federation Central Committee of the U.S. and a representative from the branch in Alexandria.

In the camp's administrative office, I saw a Jewish employer I had met on my way to Dardanelle. He suggested that I apply for a secretarial job with Mr. Fox, the representative of the camp's new workshops. I was hired and started the position with good pay. I used to work out of a small tent. Fortunately, my position with Mr. Fox didn't prevent me from continuing any of my activities with the Armenian Revolutionary Federation. My mother was also employed as a supervisor for the hospital laundry service.

***

In June, a Labor Corp was formed from people in the camp. They were sent to work at the military base of Port Said. Since the men of Musa Dagh were used to living freely, they never got quite get used to the military's strict discipline. The leading officer was strict and would lash any disobedient men, as was customary for the British military. The men rebelled and organized strikes. When they were ordered to work by the use of force, they beat the officer and returned to the camp. Thus, this effort turned out to be hopeless. Before this, another request had been made to move the men to Thessaloniki, but that had failed too.

On September 23, the supervisor of Sisuan School, Mr. H. Yeramian, and Hrachya Pehrizian moved to Alexandria to take on administrative positions at the Armenian school there.

After the collapse of the British workers' platoon in Port Said, the authorities searched for new ways to employ the men from Musa Dagh. They started talks with the French to form volunteer troops with the men. I cite an excerpt from Mr. Adom Takvorian's article, "The Formation of the Armenian Legion," published in "Alyagner Yev Khlyagner."

The glory of the formation of the Legions belongs to the deported Armenian militants of Suetia from the Port Said camps. These brave men started to apply for employment with the Allies once they arrived from Musa Dagh, mostly through the French government.

One day, the young men held a meeting and decided to send a delegation of three to the Admiral to ask for weapons. The delegation consisted of Gabriel Kazanjian, Mardiros Boyajian, and Serop Kabakian. At the meeting, Serop Kabakian, who was a formidable fighter, even begged the Admiral for weapons.

It is the effort of these illiterate but patriotic and brave men that the Armenian Legion was founded in 1916 and called for enrollment by the end of the year. The people of Suetia were the first who sent 600 militants to enlist. Noteworthy was the Battle of Arara that left a huge impact on the enemy. The battle was more than a military victory. It was a strong resistance between the light and the dark, between life and death, and ended with the destruction of the Turkish troops. Unfortunately, after three years of service, the Legion was called to cease at a time when most needed. Whatever reasons led to the decision, we respect the sacrifice of the volunteers and kiss the soil where they rest.

The Volunteer Movement

On November 19, 1916, a French military officer, Romeo, came to the campsite to register the youth of Suetia as volunteer soldiers. He invited the people to the camp center for a speech, where he spoke highly of the Musa Dagh militants. "The French government wants to take advantage of your bravery and readiness to fight," he said. With him was the French-Armenian sailor Diran Tekeyan, who had taken part in the liberation of Musa Dagh and the formation of the Armenian Legion.

On November 30, a global meeting was held at the camp, with the participation of representatives from the Armenian Revolutionary Federation, Social Democrat Hunchakian Party, and Armenian Cultural Union of Cairo.

In February 1917, the Armenian flag was blessed in the presence of Artavazd Hanemian and Stephan Yesayan, who encouraged the youth to participate in the voluntary armed movement. Artavazd Hanemian advised me to leave my current occupation and join the group, as intellectual men were also needed. I listened to Artavazd Hanemian, who I considered a voice for the Armenian Revolutionary Federation, and left my job. Together with Movses Der Kalousdian, Hovhannes Markarian, and Nareg Abrahamian, we left to Cyprus for training. There, I was appointed as a military translator and army officer.

The Volunteers in Cyprus

The coast of Monarga, or Bogazi, was our training site for seven months. All orders were given in French. Therefore, the army officers participated in weekly lectures to learn basic French and military terminology.

In the fall, our battalion was sent to gain actual fighting experience on the island of Kastellorizo, a site near the Turkish border.

The Island of Kastellorizo

The island of Kastellorizo was more like a giant mountain of stone. The island didn't have natural flowing water sources. Instead, there were man-made reservoirs that conveyed water to the city.

After we got settled, the military authorities decided to pave a road specifically for setting a cannon at the top of the mountain to bomb the Turks. The road would also help in reaching the eastern side of the island.

The island had a port and small cliff facing the Turkish border. Before the war, Greeks and Turks had lived together on the island. Now, there were only the Greek left and some spoke Turkish. There was a Greek officer who was responsible for people's basic needs and watching over the city. There were also a couple of additional armed officers. The Greek people there did not like Armenians. I didn't know where the hate stemmed from. One day, a Greek officer said to us, "A dog's coat will never be fur, and the Greeks and Armenians will never be friends." As his response, we beat him up.

Anyway, the second month of fall had arrived and we

continued paving the road. Our base was in the southern part of the city, where there was also an abandoned school. Some of our men found a drum there and it entertained us for some time.

We were ordered to relocate to the southeastern section of the island that overlooked the Turkish coast. We moved to our new site, where there was one room for the admiral and a wooden shelter for the troops.

One night, I made my way to the defense structure in the east with five of our men for guard duty. It was a very dark and cloudy night and it was imperative to be careful. We had a rapid-firing gun and two packs of ammunition with us. The structure resembled a boulder and was built with large stones covered by a tarp.

During the second shift of the night, thunder and lightning struck the sky. We were obliged to sleep outside the shelter because, much to our surprise, there were scorpions in this part of the island and they liked to stay under the rocks. As the others slept, I lay awake worrying about our fate. Halfway through the night, our youngest soldier, Aroutin, came running to wake me. "They threw a rock at us," he said.

"That is not possible since the Turkish troops are located five to 10 kilometers from the coast. Return to your location and inform me if it happens again my boy," I replied.

After a couple of moments, as I was drifting back to sleep, the young man returned to tell me it had happened again. This time, I went to see investigate. I thought to myself that the defense structure was not well-built and the coast was nearby.

"Where did the rock hit you?" I asked the other guardsman.

"It hit here, on the first flat surface," he said.

As soon as he finished showing me, something fell behind us. I went down with my gun. I found a cold rock-type mass made of ice. Quickly, I covered my gun and went back to the structure with the two guardsmen. We woke the others and got inside. As soon as we were inside, the hail started. We were fortunate that our guards had informed us. Otherwise, we could have died from the giant hail. The phone rang. It was our admiral asking about us.

Early on another morning, we went to that defense structure to get some sleep. Suddenly, one of the French army officers woke us up, shouting, "To whom did you give the weapon-cleaning oil? Son of a pig!" He was endlessly cursing. I realized that he was drunk and told him to leave us alone. He continued to shout and I was forced to punch him. The French Admiral De Marenches arrived at the scene and scolded me for punching the Frenchman. He said, "You sons of filthy Armenians are not worthy of French help. You should be punished!"

"Mon lieutenant," I said. "We are very proud of our Armenian identities. You should be ashamed of saying that, as you are a well-educated officer. We have not come here to serve the French cause. We are volunteers dedicated to the Armenian cause, which is to fight against the Turks."

"Shut up! Stand in salute position now! You are the sons of a filthy race!" the Admiral yelled.

I replied, "If that's the case, then I rescind my oath as your volunteer. Be wary that my health is not in its optimal condition. Please send me to the city tomorrow for medical testing."

"Beware! If your doctor says you're fit to serve, you'll be sent to court for being rebellious," the Admiral said.

"If I ever go to court, I will prove that I am not the son of a filthy people."

The Admiral sensed that the situation had gone too far and said, "Go, let's see what the doctor tells you."

The next day, I went to the city doctor who asked me, smiling, "What is wrong with you, my son?"

I told him that I had suffered a bullet injury on left on my temple during the resistance of Musa Dagh. Ever since the injury, when I got a little tired, I would experience panic attacks.

After a short exam, the doctor wrote in his small notebook, "15 days of rest."

Despite that, I continued my military service.

Returning to Cyprus

In December, another military group came to replace us and we returned to Cyprus.

One day, one of our compatriots from Khodr Bey, Comrade Khacher Doumanian, who was the official translator for the Legion, approached me and wanted to know why I had been tested at the medical center in Kastellorizo. I explained what had happened and he said, "Dear friend, your medical report was sent here to the central office. Upon reviewing it, Colonel Romeo advised performing a second exam on you."

After the results of the second exam, the Colonel ordered for me to withdraw from physical training and be employed in the military office. I handed over my gun and worked in the office for some time. I used to think to myself how reckless it had been to get involved in the volunteer movement.

In January 1918, Colonel Romeo terminated my contract and sent me to Port Said the following day. In one day, I went from being a military professional to a civil man. I knew the reason behind the sudden termination was the ill-mannered Admiral De Marenches.

***

I went to Alexandria where my sister lived. I searched for employment in the British army of Palestine but had no luck. Five weeks passed without employment. Finally, on April 10, I found a job. I was employed in the British and Foreign Bible Society, with the help of Mr. Mihran Siraganian, my sister's husband. I became a secretary for the location in Port Said. I used to visit the camp every Saturday to see my mother and fiancée, Miss Dirouhi Nkrourian. And so, my life returned to a normal routine.

Meanwhile, the Armenian Legion, together with the American volunteers, passed through Port Said on their way to Palestine. That day, a special ceremony was held and Archbishop Torkom Koushagian blessed the liberation flag that the Musa Daghians had used.

Ceasefire, November 11, 1918

World War I ended on November 11, 1918 with a ceasefire. The Armenians living in Port Said went to the British and French embassies to congratulate them.

On November 28, an open meeting was held at the camp with many present. The speakers were Mr. Mardig Der Sahagian from the Armenian Cultural Union, Archimandrite Mampre Sirounian, and Pastor Antreassian. During the meeting, people got very enthusiastic and suggested sending a letter to the leader of the French delegation, Boghos Noubar Pasha. The letter would request for him to become the mediator representing the 8000 refugees and militant men of Musa Dagh to the French government. The aim would be to raise awareness for the

Armenian cause and form a united Armenia again.

Here, I reference excerpts from Hrant Samuel's article, "The Glorious Winner of Arara," written on the occasion of the heroic Battle of Arara,

From one side, the Armenian people were fighting a war of life and death at the front of the Caucasus. On the other side, the youth of America and Egypt were registering themselves as volunteer fighters, aiming to create the Eastern Legion in Cyprus which was later called the Armenian Legion. The majority of the fighters in this Legion were the brave men of Musa Dagh.

This Legion's work was to later be written in Armenian history books as heroic and exemplary.

The militants of the Legion used to perform their military training to the "Cilicia" song. They were sent to the front of Palestine to take part in the attacks under Marshal Allenby, which was to start on September 18.

They were able to conquer the once unapproachable location of Arara, sacrificing 23 brave martyrs and 70 injured men. During the battle, one would see the injured men encouraging the fighters to take their revenge.

Following the battle, on September 20, the 23 martyrs were buried. During the ceremony, the obituary speech was given by the head officer of the Legion, Colonel Romeo. The Colonel spoke,

The Armenian heroes fell victim to their enemy with the utmost bravery. All of them deserve the war cross and all of them are defenders and saints of the Legion. Rest in peace and glory! You paved the way towards justice and the recognition of your rights that were forgotten for centuries. I vow, in front of your graves, that you will be truly and completely compensated.

On October 12, 1918, Marshal Allenby, the head of the Allied forces of Palestine, sent a letter to the president of the National Delegation of Paris, Boghos Noubar Pasha, glorifying the Armenian Legion, "I am proud to have an Armenian military unit under my command. They fought heroically and had a huge positive impact on the result of the battle."

After the battle of Arara, the road was open. The British cavalry raced across the Mediterranean Coast towards Haifa, then towards Nazareth, surprising Liman von Sanders Pasha who fled to Tiberias.

After some time, the members of the Legion arrived in Cilicia, by way of Lebanon and Syria.

Fifty years after the Battle of Arara, we sadly announce that the Allies forgot the promises they made to their minor allies. They denied the Armenian cause and their promises for compensation.

The 23 heroes of Arara currently rest in their graves in Jerusalem, where they were transported on April 24, 1974. The ceremony of their transportation was guided by Patriarch Yeghishe Tourian.

Rest in peace my beloved heroes. Your nation will be proud of your accomplishment and never forget the sacrifices you made for your motherland.

***

On October 2, 1919, a meeting was held at the Armenian camps of Port Said under the chairmanship of Dr. M. Salpy. The meeting's purpose was to address the Armenian Republic's May 28 Act. The meeting culminated in a letter to the chairman of the Armenian Parliament,

Dear Mr. Avedis Aharonian,
Chairman of the Armenian Parliament, Paris,

On behalf of the fighters of Musa Dagh, the soldiers of the Armenian Legion, heroes of Arara, and more than 3,000 Armenian refugees, I request for you to communicate our gratitude and appreciation to your parliament regarding the May 28 Act.

Chairperson of the meeting,
Dr. M. Salpy

Mr. A. Aharonian had replied to the letter as such, "We are especially honored to receive this message from the brave fighters who immortalized the Armenian name on Mount Arara, just like the brave Armenians who fought for the current Armenian Republic."

Four Years Later (1919)

Armenians survived the horrid talons of the Armenian Genocide by the will of God. From July 31, 1919, to October, around 3000 people from Musa Dagh started their journey back to their ancestral homes. By the end of November, the camp of Port Said no longer existed.

In April 1919, my family and I moved to Beirut by boat. Two days later, we went to Aleppo, where the British and Foreign

Bible Society had transferred my position. We stayed in Aleppo for a whole year.

My brother Armenag, who had been released from the voluntary troops, came to reunite with us in Aleppo. He told us about the life of militants in Cilicia and, specifically, Adana. He seemed to have lost his hope.

After staying with us for a few months, he went to Urfa to find what remained of my maternal uncle. He found that Mustafa Kemal Ataturk's influence had already reached Urfa. After being held captive for some time, in April 1920, my brother was killed in a gorge outside of Urfa.

1920 was a very tragic year for our family. On the first days of January, when my sister Aznive, was in Addis Ababa, Ethiopia with her husband, she died while giving birth in the hospital. Ten days later, the child also died.

I left my job and headed to Beirut with my mother. After staying there for a couple of months, we returned to Port Said by boat. Misfortune struck again. One morning, when I was biking to work, my leg got caught under an Egyptian man's chariot who was in the British military. Nevertheless, I recovered smoothly.

In August 1921, my mother went to Musa Dagh and returned with my fiancée, Dirouhi. We got married. Those next three years were a relatively peaceful time in my life.

In 1925, I visited Musa Dagh and took some photographs of the battle locations. Later, a monument was constructed there and a special opening ceremony was held. For the ceremony, the following letter was sent to Admiral Dartige du Fournet.

Khodr Bey, Musa Dagh

19 September 1932

To Mr. Admiral Dartige du Fournet
Mr. Admiral,

You may think that your noble support that rescued the inhabitants of Musa Dagh has been forgotten or is not appreciated. However, deep in our hearts, we shall never forget that generosity. This monument built by the people of Musa Daghians represents our sentiments. You are a celebrated liberator. When the construction of this monument was decided, the inhabitants were living under tough circumstances and preoccupied with rebuilding their destroyed homes. However, they never forgot about their liberator and built the monument stone by stone.

The opening for the monument took place on September 18 and was held by Vice Admiral Juber, who represented the French navy. We would be very pleased to have you at our opening celebration.

Your name is engraved, not only on the monument but, inside each Musa Daghian's heart.

Please accept our utmost blessings,
Monument Committee
Chairperson of the Committee
S. Tossounian

The following is the sentence engraved on the monument,

To the French Navy,
After resisting the enemy and defending their rights, the Armenians of Musa Dagh were rescued by a French ship from Syria whose leader was Vice Admiral Dartige du Fournet. September 1915

3 October 1932 The Admiral replied,
Villa Paknam, Périgueux, France

Mr. S. Tossounian
Chairperson of the Musa Dagh Monument, Khodr Bey,

The letter sent by the Armenians of Musa Dagh for the occasion of the monument's opening on September 18 was very heartfelt.

I am touched by your words and particular thankfulness towards me. I was proud to read my name engraved on the monument that will immortalize your resistance during the hard days of 1915. I assure you that the Third Fleet and, in particular, the gracious soul of Admiral Dario will be forever grateful to have taken part in this act.

Having heard that the Armenians of Musa Dagh have returned to their ancestral villages and rebuilt what had been damaged, please send my best wishes for happiness and peace.

Let them remember in their prayers, the French navy and the old admiral that will never forget the Armenians of Musa Dagh.

Accept my best wishes for success,
Vice Admiral
Dartige du Fournet

***

My job with the British and Foreign Bible Society would be cause for me to travel from Beirut to Syria at times. We had a collection of books in Antioch and Iskenderun, and a bookstore in Aleppo and Damascus. Taking advantage of one of my visits, I went to Antioch and Iskenderun for the last time. I also visited Kesab and the village of Yoghunoluk in Musa Dagh.

Another time, I went to Iskenderun by sea, intending to

take photos of Musa Dagh. The missionary of Iskenderun was a polite man. We were having lunch together and discussing the present state of affairs when he said,

I will give a piece of advice to you and the people of Musa Dagh. Be certain that Mustafa Kemal Ataturk, who successfully abandoned the Allied forces from Cilicia, will try to conquer Sanjak also. What will happen to the people of Musa Dagh? Turkey cannot forget its defeat on your lands. Go to your village and sell your property before it's too late.

In spring 1935, I was commanded to go to Aleppo and welcome a British missionary who was going to arrive from London by railway. The woman arrived that day and wanted us to travel to Qamishli using the Aleppo-Baghdad railway. I didn't want to take that route so she went by train and I took a bus that was going to pass through Deir ez-Zor. Mr. Movses Borounsezian, a bookseller from Aleppo, accompanied me as well.

The bus driver was an Armenian from Syria so I requested for him to show us some of the specific sites where Armenian deportees had passed during the Genocide. The bus passed through Meskene and Raqqa before reaching Deir ez-Zor. There, I watched in tears as we drove past the bridge over the Euphrates River that hundreds of deportees had crossed during the Genocide. I had also asked the driver to go through the deserts where we could see human bones scattered all over the ground. In the evening, we passed through that horrid scene in the moonlight, the black ghost of the Genocide passing before my tearful eyes.

To Lebanon

In the spring of 1925, we moved to Beirut. I was still working for the British and Foreign Bible Society. After having lived in Port Said, the Armenian hub of Beirut seemed very pleasant to me. There, I saw relatives from Urfa who reminded me of old memories.

A year later, we founded the Armenian Association of Urfa. Although this association didn't belong to any political party, members of the Armenian Revolutionary Federation made up its majority. We put a lot of effort into preserving the Armenian culture and advancing the educational system.

At that time, I hadn't transferred my Armenian Revolutionary Federation membership to Beirut but I continued to donate as I could. This caught the attention of some narrowminded and sour people from the church who inquired whether I was a member of the Armenian Revolutionary Federation. I let them know that Armenian Revolutionary Federation members were not as faithless as they believed and, thereafter, kept my distance.

Despite this, I worked for seven years in the principal Protestant church as a secretary and treasurer. The Pastor was Y. Hadidian, who used to preach in Turkish because most of the church attendees were from Cilicia. This sparked a powerful protest which caused the language to change to Armenian.

The years flew by. God granted our family another son and daughter and we became a large family. We also had our own house.

After a period of peace, misfortune struck again through jealousy. Some of the clerical men wrote letters to the British and Foreign Bible Society saying that I was intermixing my nationalist views with the church and disrespecting the church. So, I left the job to start my own business.

Since starting a business in Beirut was tough, I went to Cairo with my friend from Musa Dagh, Setrag Boursalian, to explore what kind of business I could start. I planned to move to Cairo with my family.

To Cairo

In May 1939, after returning to Beirut and settling all of our affairs, we moved to Cairo. Two of my children went to the Kalousdian Armenian School, while one went to the American girl's college near our house.

Life was normal again. However, I was never able to get used to the weather in Cairo and I developed joint pains. My family doctor, Yervant Khatanassian, told me, "You are from Musa Dagh. Without any hesitation, you should return to Lebanon and find work outdoors before your joint pain worsens."

In May 1939, we returned to Beirut. That same year, World War II began and we gave up the idea of living in Beirut.

Anjar

During this time, the Armenians of Musa Dagh decided to leave their beloved mountain and migrated, in groups, to Anjar, located on the Beqaa fields of Lebanon near the Syrian border.

The circumstances in Anjar were not favorable. A second campsite was built and inhabited by Armenians. During that fall and winter, the people stayed in canvas tents and many died. However, the people from the mountain survived until the French government built a room and a bathroom. The people started to organize. They started small businesses and opened schools. Some sanitary procedures were put in place and people were vaccinated for yellow fever.

During World War II, when France was defeated by the Germans, the British army attacked Lebanon over Palestine and conquered it. Some offices were constructed in the military bases. We used to live in Zahle, where I had managed to find a job in the Ablah military unit as an auditor. I was in charge of auditing the finances and inventory. My daughter, Aznive was the typist there.

This was the state of things until the ceasefire of 1946. Then, we were obliged to move because the Ablah military base was officially transferred to Beirut. In 1941, we had sold our house and bought property in Chtaura, where I had planned to construct a new house. This became a reason for me to study agriculture and, in particular, fruit trees and gardening. At least this new venture helped relieve my joint pain.

***

The Armenians of Musa Dagh finally settled in Anjar, which was later called Haush Musa. The new villages there were named after the six villages from Musa Dagh.

In 1940, I took the initiative to build ovens. The villages of Musa Dagh had their own tonir ovens but it proved very difficult to implement the same system in Anjar. The undertaking seemed hopeful until it became impossible to find flour.

At that time, through the efforts of Krikor Koudouyan from Zeitun, an Armenian village was built in Zahle. Some people from Beirut, like Comrade Nigol Aghpalian, Hagop Uvezian,

Sisag Manougian, Derounian (a photographer), and others purchased summer country houses there. It was a pleasant environment in this Armenian village. For example, Mr. Uvezian held a musical concert there. Also, during the nights, one could hear young people singing.

Aside from his village house, Comrade Nigol Aghpalian bought another area of land next to mine. When he would pass by our house, he used to greet us. One day, my wife invited him over.

"Comrade Abadjian," he said to me. "Are you aware that you are an intimidating man?"

"In what way?" I asked him.

We call those who own huge properties intimidating," he had replied. It was pleasant to converse with Comrade Aghpalian.

It was the last month of summer. I wanted to give him some of my grapes. As I approached his house, I saw him sitting with his hands on his head. He was asleep but awoke when he heard my footsteps.

"Welcome, come in. Let's have a cup of coffee,"

he told me.

"Comrade Aghpalian, since you called me 'intimidating' because of my property, I wanted to give you some of my grapes," I told him.

"Excuse my expression, but I wish for all Armenians to be 'intimidating' towards our enemies. I have seen so many things and look at where we are now, away from our ancestral motherland! The other day, when you asked me to give you one of my properties for rent, I agreed on the condition that you didn't cultivate roses there. You know why? My relatives used to cultivate roses in Armenia and I don't want to revive old memories." Comrade Aghpalian's eyes filled with tears and I didn't ask further questions.

In 1947, repatriation to the Armenian Republic in the Soviet Union had begun. One day, some of my friends asked me to guide them to Comrade Aghpalian's residence for advice about repatriating to Armenia. We found him sitting on his chair as usual. His advice was, "You are going to your motherland and not just any land. Don't ever think twice and don't be affected by the current regime. When the situation improves, Armenia will open its doors to everyone."

That year was full of surprises. We had the privilege of meeting some friends from Egypt, such as Khacher Guezelimanian and Dr. Hamo Ohanchanian. I was fortunate to give them my grapes as well. Comrade Arshag Hovhanessian also visited with his wife and rented a room in our house for the summer.

Twenty years later, as I write about these memories, I recall a lot of good times.

***

In January 1946, I planned a visit to Egypt to see relatives and friends. I passed through Jerusalem on my way back and stayed with Mihran Siraganian, my sister's husband. Gassia, my daughter, was a nurse in the hospital of Jerusalem. At that time the Arab-Israeli conflict had already begun.

I was considering immigrating to South America. I also researched moving to Canada and sent an application to Ottawa. At the same time, I applied for immigration to Australia. After a couple of months, I received rejections because of our Armenian origins.

In the meantime, 150 people from Musa Dagh applied for repatriation to Armenia. In the fall of 1947, I rented two rooms in Achrafieh. After losing all hopes of immigrating to Canada, I wrote a letter to my friend in Venezuela to grant us entry to the country. In 1948, we were granted permission.

During that time, my daughter, Gassia, had managed to leave Jerusalem and stayed with us for a while. She then went to London to continue her studies in nursing. My youngest daughter, Arpine, graduated from the British girl's school in Beirut. In June, when we were returning from her graduation ceremony, my mother fell from the chariot and injured her leg. We took her to the hospital but sadly she didn't survive. She had already felt that she would be unable to accompany us to South America. "I will travel somewhere else, my dear," she used to say. In July 1948, she left us for good.

After the loss of my mother, it was time to permanently leave the Near East, where I had spent the memorable and pleasant days of my youth.

To A New World

We were granted permission to enter Venezuela through our friend Comrade Levon Kouyoumjian. After settling all of our matters, we traveled through New York to Caracas, the capital city of Venezuela.

To Venezuela

Anyone setting foot in Venezuela for the first time wants to return right back to where they came from.

Before 1950, the Armenians of Venezuela were less than 100

in number. Among them was the Dzaghigian family who had become very rich. Stepan Dzaghigian, in particular, helped each and every Armenian arriving to Venezuela.

Mr. Houlian was another man from Musa Dagh who was happy to see fellow Armenians and speak in his dialect. On the first New Year, he hosted a celebration and invited all of the Armenians. I remember he said, "I am very grateful to see Armenians finally arriving to Venezuela. I was very worried that I would assimilate here and forget the Armenian language."

There was also a doctor from Armenia. He had been taken captive during World War II after which he had gone to Germany, then to the Mekhitarists of Venice, and eventually to Venezuela. Although I knew him well, he didn't speak much of his past. During World War I, he had served as a doctor in Yerznga with the Armenian voluntary troops. He spoke with great discontent about the Russian retreat because it had hurt their progress.

***

I was permitted to Venezuela as an expert in tree planting, and so I was searching for a place to do so in the capital. Unfortunately, my certificate in agriculture from the Lebanese government had been left at the agricultural office. Just a few months after our arrival, the first revolution started and the military took over the government. As a result, my case was neglected and I was left unemployed. I had practiced some photography during my youth and I used it to make some money for family expenses.

My two youngest daughters, came to Caracas with their nursing degrees. Gassia had British citizenship and only stayed in Latin America for six months. Thereafter, she chose to head to Canada for work. She was the reason we all went to Canada some years later. Eventually, Arpine also went to Canada to live with Gassia in the city of London, located in Ontario.

My son, Mardig, took special classes in telecommunication after graduating from school in Caracas. However, he had a difficult time adjusting to the culture so I invited him to work in our photography shop. After some months, we noticed that Mardig had a talent for photography. Day by day, he took over the ownership and management of our shop.

My wife, my son, and I stayed in Acarigua for five years. As my son Mardig completely took over the photography shop, I worked part-time as a private teacher for Spanish-speakers. This helped bring in extra income.

In 1960, we went to Canada to attend Arpines's wedding. I stayed for three months. For my return, I had to go to Montreal for paperwork and this gave me an opportunity to visit the capital, Ottawa, with my daughters.

***

Day after day, I grew more aware that the governmental structure of the Latin American countries wasn't designed for success, although one could make a living. Life was always unstable.

Therefore, we chose to spend the last part of our lives in Canada.

To Canada, Our Final Stop

In fall 1961, we left Acarigua, Venezuela and headed to Canada. We visited New York, Boston, and Worcester and were hosted by Comrade Mardiros Kazanjian and Der Movses Shirikian from Musa Dagh.

On September 17, 1961 we were welcomed in Toronto by my daughters and grandchildren.

***

We shouldn't be afraid of losing the Armenian culture. The risk of assimilating would be very low if we maintained the Armenian language and customs. In efforts to do just that, the Armenian Orthodox Church in Canada held Armenian classes on Saturdays. The educational council invited me to teach advanced classes there. It was with great pleasure that I taught there for two years.

The Armenian Relief Society and the Hamazkayin Armenian Educational and Cultural Society also put all of their efforts into Armenian cultural maintenance.

Disappearing Faces

Before ending this memoir, I want to remember some of the important faces from my life's journey who have since left this world.

Pastor Dikran Antreassian

I write this on September 12, two years after Pastor Dikran Antreassian's death. This date takes me back to 1915, when the Armenians were saved by the French navy. Half a century has passed since the Genocide. That year became a historical one that will never be forgotten by the Armenian Nation. The Genocide of 1915 took 1.5 million Armenian souls. Despite that tragedy, we also had heroic battles and resistance, of which Musa Dagh is noteworthy.

At the beginning of the Musa Dagh resistance, Pastor Antreassian led by example by moving his family to the mountain. There, he had a huge impact organizing and leading the resistance. He wasn't a member of a political party but he always advised the militants to follow orders and fight. He could have occupied high positions and taken many roles in South America but he preferred to stay next to the Armenian people. He served for 40 years in the villages of Musa Dagh and churches of Kesab and Aleppo.

In 1915, he gave a lecture at Egypt's American mission and it was later published as an English-language booklet. Evidently, Franz Werfel used some stories from this booklet to write the famous book, "The Forty Days of Musa Dagh." He was a true intellectual whose memoirs and writings became essential resources in Armenian history. Among them was

"The Deportation of Zeitun and the Resistance of Suetia." He was very eager to preserve the rules of written Armenian. In his speeches, he always mentioned the importance of preserving our Armenian identities and our cultural responsibility. He died in Beirut at the age of 74. Are the Armenian people proud of Armenians like him?

May we honor his unforgettable legacy.

Dikran Ardouni (Eurdoghlian)

Dikran Ardouni was born in 1885, in Marash. In 1891, he moved to Urfa. He survived the Hamidian massacres of 1895. At the age of 23, he graduated from the American "Central Turkey" College in Aintab and returned to Urfa as a teacher. After that, he was sent to Constantinople, where he graduated from the agricultural college.

He was ordered to serve in the Turkish army as a vice admiral and sent to the Albanian front. During World War I, his family was deported and his two brothers, Francis and Joseph, died in battle in the village of Garmouj, near Urfa.

He witnessed the deportation of the intellectuals of Constantinople during the Genocide. During those days, he also met the revolutionary leader Dikran Dzamhour.

He stayed in the Turkish army until 1918, when the Allies conquered Afyonkarahisar. He then moved to Cilicia and was admitted to the French Armed Forces with the help of an Armenian Revolutionary Federation leader named Gaian. In France, he continued to resist Mustafa Kemal Ataturk's agenda but became hopeless upon witnessing the French shift their relations with them.

Hagop Uvezian

Hagop Uvezian was born on 1891, in Marash. As a child, he loved singing and playing musical instruments. During the years of 1912 and 1913, he was my teacher at the American "Central Turkey" College in Aintab. In 1913, he went to Geneva to pursue higher education. He wrote many nationalist songs and performed musical concerts for Armenians and foreigners.

He died in Beirut on February 5, 1943. H. Varjabedian memorialized him in the "Azdarar" by describing him as "the man who was born a musician and died a musician." Before leaving Lebanon, I visited his grave and saw the following engraving, "Here rests musician Hagop Uvezian, an Armenian from Marash. Do you hear the melody of the wildflowers resting on my grave? 1891-1943, Hagop Uvezian."

Nigol Aghpalian

I cannot leave Nigol Aghpalian out of my memoir. He was an intellectual with vast knowledge. I used to attend his lectures in Beirut but never had the chance to discuss them with him in person.

In 1940, Hagop Uvezian performed music in the hall of the Protestant church of Chtaura. When the "Yerevan Etudes" started to play, I noticed Nigol Aghpalian wiping tears away. What was he thinking of? Why was he so sad?

One day, we were at our house in Chtaura. He said to me, "This humble village may become an Armenian cultural hub, though I don't know if I'll live to see it."

He died on the 15th of August. One morning, they found him dead on the floor, on his way to the kitchen. He was fully dressed, as if preparing for an eternal journey. Thousands walked after his coffin headed for the cemetery of Furn el Chebbak. The Lebanese used to say that "Armenians were burying their king." No one ever forgets Nigol Aghpalian, who died away from the motherland with his soul and life dedicated to it. May we honor his unforgettable legacy.

Haroutioun Manougian

Haroutioun Manougian was born in 1914 in Kharpert. He later moved to Lebanon with his mother, brother, and sister.

His father, Samuel, was killed by Turks. He and his brother went on to pursue higher education. The eldest, Antranig, became the chief doctor of the mental hospital of Beirut, while Haroutioun studied agriculture. In 1960, he settled in Canada. He was an exemplar, serving the Armenian Revolutionary Federation both in Beirut and Toronto. In 1962, I saw him again in Toronto. "I am Haroutioun," he said, "Do you remember?" The child that I remembered was now a mature young man.

He was always ready to serve the Armenian community of Canada. Unfortunately, after two years there, he died. We buried him on January 25, 1964. I read his obituary at the funeral,

My dear friend, I saw your smiling face yesterday. You walked the path of eternal service. In our sorrow, we find hope in your memory, that there are other Armenians like you who will continue the work of past revolutionaries.

Israel Seferian

In the year 1969, the Armenian Revolutionary Federation lost two members. One of them was Comrade Hagop Mouradian, and the other was Comrade Israel Seferian. I want to mention some details about Israel's life. He was born in Mush in 1878. In 1906, he went to Constantinople and then, in 1907, to the United States. In 1923, when he had lost all hope of the survival of his wife and two children, he married Yerchanig Simonian. Vrej, his son, later became a professor.

In intimate settings, he used to tell stories from his life in Mush. He would tell of the Mush villagers' pilgrimage to the Saint Garabed Monastery.

Later, along with his brothers Abel and Daniel, he pledged allegiance to the Armenian Revolutionary Federation. Comrade Israel was a vehement member of the Armenian Revolutionary Federation.

To those that it interests, I would like to share some specific stories from Israel's life. Every year on May 28, the date of independence for Armenia's first republic, he used to display the Armenian flag from his balcony in Canada. One day, a Canadian officer noticed the large Armenian flag and the small Canadian flag hanging from his balcony. He knocked on his door and said, "I'd like to know what country that flag belongs to.

Israel replied, "Oh! You must have never heard or read about Armenians. Are you aware that we've existed for thousands of years? Noah's Ark settled on Mount Ararat of Armenia!"

"I understand. But why is the Armenian flag larger than the Canadian flag?" the officer asked.

"Because we existed a long time ago, before the appearance of the New World."

Another time, at his grandson's baptism, when the priest asked him to recite the traditional phrase, he answered. "Sword, weapon, and the Armenian Revolutionary Federation." The priest explained how the sentence was actually "Faith, hope, and love." Israel answered, "Yes, but I have promised what I can offer and he can manage the rest."

Let us not forget his life.
December 20, 1969, Toronto

Ms Karina Shatek

Ms Karina Shatek was a missionary who served Armenians from 1876 until she moved to Urfa. In Urfa, she founded the girls' college. After witnessing the Hamidian massacres of 1895, she dedicated herself to the orphans. After the 1909 massacre of Cilicia, she became very weak. In 1910, she returned to her birthplace in America and died.

Ms M. Frearson

In 1897, Ms M. Frearson served as a missionary in Marash and, later, in Aintab. Until the dark days of 1915, she used to run an orphanage. In 1918, she served Armenian refugees in Egypt. She later settled in the Lebanese village of Shemlan. In 1947, she was bedridden due to a heart attack and died three years later. There must be a lot of survivors today who remember her as their mother.

***

Over the course of my life, I have met many people with different viewpoints and taken part in several movements. As a result, I have arrived at the belief that success for Armenians lies in a political ideology that unites all of our forces, especially when we have so many exemplary heroes to learn from.

My memoir is scattered pages from 75 years of my life and may serve as a resource for future historians. Nevertheless, I will find the utmost fulfillment if, at the very least, my memoir echoes our experiences to future generations.

Hagop Abadjian, Cyprus 1917

Translators From left, Nikola Nigokhosian, Movses Kheyoian, Hagop Abadjian. October 10, 1915

Port Said, Egypt 1918

Mardiros Abadjian

Abadjian family
Aznive, Armenag, Hagop
and their Mother

Abadjian siblings Aznive and Hagop
Urfa 1914

Doctor on French Navy Cruiser, Guishen
September 1915
This photograph was always with Abadjian and was found in his pocket
when he passed away in 1983

French Navy Cruiser, Guishen

Port Said campsite Labour Corp volunteers sitting, from left Ms. Mari,
M.s Cunnington, Mr. Fox, Ms. Ferirson, H. Abadjian.
1916

Port Said, Egypt 1917

French Servicemen, Cyprus 1917

Camp Souedia, Cyprus 1917

Dirouhi Abadjian

Hagop and Dirouhi Abadjian
Port Said, Egypt August 11, 1921

Abadjians children, oldest to youngest
Aznive, Gassia, Arpineh and Mardiros.
Beirut

Survivors return to visit Musa Dagh, 1931

With daughters Arpineh and Gassia
Egypt

Abadjian and his son on a ship to
New York

Arrived in Venezuela
1948

With 13 yr old son Mardiros.
Venezuela 1948

Gassia in nursing school
London, England

Dirouhi and Aznive at their
photography studio
Acarigua, Venezuela

Hagop Abadjian
Alexandria, Egypt 1916

www.ingramcontent.com/pod-product-compliance
Lightning Source LLC
Chambersburg PA
CBHW022015290426
44109CB00015B/1177